Teacher-Directed PALS

Paths to Achieving Literacy Success:

Teacher-Directed Beginning Reading Lessons

Patricia G. Mathes, Ph.D.
Jill Howard Allor, Ed.D.
Joseph K. Torgesen, Ph.D.
Shelley H. Allen, Ph.D.

Edited by Raven Moore
Text layout by Sherri Rowe
Cover design by Sue Campbell
Production Assistance by Kimberly Harris

ISBN 1-57035-351-4

Support for the development of this manual and empirical validation of the materials it contains was provided by Grants #H023N30003 and #H180G60004 from the Office of Special Education Programs in the U.S. Department of Education. However, statements made and positions taken in this manual do not necessarily reflect the positions or policies of this funding agency, and no official endorsement should be inferred.

Printed in the United States of America

Published and Distributed by

SOPRIS WEST
EDUCATIONAL SERVICES

A Cambium Learning™ Company

4093 Specialty Place • Longmont, CO 80504 • (303) 651-2829
www.**sopris**west.com

142TDP\C&M\5-05

Acknowledgments

We thank the teachers of the Davidson County Public Schools, Nashville, Tennessee; the Leon County Public Schools, Tallahassee, Florida; and the Florida State University School for helping us to develop and validate these materials. We also thank the many graduate students both at Vanderbilt University and at Florida State University who were members of our research team.

About the Authors

Patricia G. Mathes is an educational researcher and former classroom/reading teacher who received her Ph.D. in 1992 in Education and Human Development from Peabody College of Vanderbilt University. In 1999, she joined the faculty at the University of Texas, Houston Medical School as Associate Professor of Developmental Pediatrics. At that time, she also joined the researchers affiliated with the Center for Academic and Reading Skills located at the University of Texas. She has also served on the faculties of the College of Education at Florida State University and Peabody College for Teachers at Vanderbilt University. Since 1991, she has been conducting large-scale, classroom-based reading intervention research with funding from multiple sources, including the U.S. Department of Education, the National Institute of Child Health and Human Development, the National Science Foundation, and state agencies. She is the author of numerous articles, chapters, and books related to learning and reading disabilities, accommodating academic diversity, and best practices for struggling readers. Dr. Mathes serves on the editorial boards of four scholarly journals and provides nationwide teacher/staff development focused on translating research into practice.

Jill Howard Allor is an educational researcher and former classroom teacher who received her Ed.D. in 1996 from Peabody College at Vanderbilt University in Special Education with an emphasis in reading development. In 1998 she joined the faculty of Louisiana State University in the Department of Curriculum and Instruction. Her work there focuses on special education and early literacy. She has also served as a research associate and adjunct professor at Florida State University, where she coordinated large-scale, classroom-based reading intervention research. She has conducted research funded through the U.S. Office of Education, focusing on early intervention and the role of phonological processing in reading acquisition. She has provided teacher/staff development on various topics including peer tutoring, early literacy development, phonemic awareness instruction, literacy assessment, and other literacy instructional techniques.

Joseph K. Torgesen received his Ph.D. in Developmental and Clinical Psychology from the University of Michigan in 1976. He is currently appointed as Distinguished Research Professor of Psychology and Education at Florida State University. He has been conducting research with children who have learning problems for 25 years and has authored over 140 articles, book chapters, books, and tests related to reading and learning disabilities. He also serves on the editorial boards of five research journals. For the past 12 years, Dr. Torgesen has been part of the effort supported by the National Institute of Child Health and Human Development to learn more about the nature of reading disabilities and ways to prevent and remediate reading problems in children. For the past five years, he has been actively involved in trying to help teachers and other professionals incorporate the findings from recent research into classroom practice.

Shelley H. Allen earned her Ph.D. from Ohio State University in 1994, specializing in children's literature, elementary language arts, and classroom discourse. She has taught elementary school as well as university-level courses in language arts and children's literature. She has also worked as a research associate and later as a project coordinator for large-scale, reading-related research projects at Peabody College for Teachers at Vanderbilt University. She has authored a book chapter, co-authored journal articles, and presented papers at national conferences. She currently stays at home full-time, sharing her love of children's books with her young son.

Contents

Preface

The materials and procedures found in this manual have been built on the work of many others. The Sounds and Words activities are based on Direct Instruction principles and borrow Direct Instruction formats (Carnine, Silbert, & Kameenui, 1997). Those versed in the Direct Instruction model will also recognize that we have adhered to principles of Direct Instruction in determining the order in which new information is presented. Likewise, in developing the Story Sharing routine we were influenced by principles of guided reading (Fountas & Pinnell, 1996).

CHAPTER ONE:
What is *Teacher-Directed PALS?*

An Overview

Teacher-Directed PALS is a curriculum for beginning or struggling readers, designed to be used by individuals who are not necessarily experts in how to teach reading, but who want to help beginning or struggling readers learn to read better. (Please note: This book uses the term "Teacher" to refer to any individual who is providing reading instruction, with or without teacher certification and credentials. Likewise, this book uses the term "student" to refer to any beginning or struggling reader who is working with this program.)

Originally designed as a research intervention to compliment *Peer-Assisted Literacy Strategies for First Grade Readers* (Mathes, Torgesen, & Allen, 2000), *Teacher-Directed PALS* was designed specifically to be used by paraprofessionals and teachers working with small groups (1-3 students) of struggling readers (Mathes & Babyak, in press). However, it has also been successfully used in classrooms in which *First Grade PALS* was not being implemented (Mathes, Torgesen, & Menchetti, 2000).

Used as a supplemental curriculum for struggling beginning readers who need an additional boost in learning how to read, *Teacher-Directed PALS* has been used successfully by teachers, adult volunteers, and paraprofessionals working within classroom settings. It has also been used as the curriculum for America Reads (a U.S. Department of Education reading initiative, in which college students tutor

school age-children) in several sites across the U.S.

Why *Teacher-Directed PALS* is Effective: The Research Base

Over the past 30 years, researchers of reading have been very active in the study of literacy acquisition, and much is now known about how to prevent reading difficulties in students who come to school with a variety of risk factors (Brown & Felton, 1990; Foorman, Francis, Fletcher, Schatschneider, & Mehta, 1998; Torgesen, 1997; Torgesen, Wagner, & Rashotte, 1997; Vellutino et al., 1996). Converging evidence from studies like those just cited suggests that with appropriate instruction nearly all students, including those from low-income backgrounds or with mild disabilities, can become competent readers. Thus, this book's authors believe that one of education's most important present challenges is how to balance the various aspects of what is known in ways that are both practical for teachers and responsive to the unique learning needs of individual students. Included in this balance must be provisions for (1) early identification of children at risk for reading failure; (2) carefully designed intense early reading instruction incorporating systematic, explicit instruction in alphabetic reading skills balanced with meaningful experiences with children's literature and writing; and (3) continued support beyond the initial acquisition of reading skill to ensure continued academic growth into the upper grades (Mathes & Torgesen, 1998). *Teacher-Directed PALS* is specifically designed to address the need for systematic and explicit instruction in alphabetic reading, balanced with extensive practice in reading of children's literature.

Helping Struggling Readers

Evidence indicates that students who are likely to experience reading failure share the same basic needs for literacy instruction as higher performing readers do (Langenberg & Associates, 2000; Mathes & Torgesen, 1998; Snow, Burns, & Griffen, 1998). What sets these struggling learners apart from higher performing learners is that systematic, explicit instruction appears to be **critical** rather than merely beneficial, and that struggling readers require **more instructional time** and more **opportunities to practice** (Torgesen, 1998). *Teacher-Directed PALS* incorporates this critical systematic, explicit instructional content and is designed to be delivered in small groups or in tutorials in addition to other reading instruction. Thus, if used appropriately, *Teacher-Directed PALS* provides students with more instructional time working on critical content, and its instructional format allows each individual student more opportunities to practice this critical content.

Rather than waiting for students to fail, this book's authors believe that risk should be assessed upon students' entry into school, and intervention (which can include *Teacher-Directed PALS*) begun before failure has occurred (Foorman, Francis, Shaywitz, Shaywitz, & Fletcher, 1997; Foorman, Francis, Winikates, Mehta, Schatschneider, & Fletcher, 1997). Likewise, because *Teacher-Directed PALS* is

designed to be used by paraprofessionals or other adult tutors/volunteers, it represents a relatively low-cost vehicle for delivering the critical content and practice to those students who require it.

The Critical Content

For students who experience difficulty in learning to read, research points to the need to provide instruction that includes provisions for readers to develop phonemic awareness, letter knowledge, and the skills required to combine phonetic decoding strategies with contextual constraints in order to accurately identify novel words in print (National Research Council, 1998; Share & Stanovich, 1995). This instruction needs to directly address the acquisition of accurate and quick word recognition skills, speed and ease of reading text, extensive engagement with children's literature, and strategies for enhancing the deep understanding of text (National Research Council, 1998). *Teacher-Directed PALS* addresses these needs in several ways, as discussed following.

Word Recognition

Most crucial among the critical components of a curriculum for beginning at-risk readers is the inclusion of systematic instruction in word recognition, which includes building foundational phonemic awareness skills (Torgesen & Mathes, 2000). Extensive research over the past two decades has produced a strong consensus among researchers that the fundamental problem for most students who experience serious difficulty learning to read involves problems in acquiring accurate and fluent word identification skills; these problems subsequently interfere with comprehension development (Chard, Simmons, & Kameenui, 1995; Foorman, 1995; Stanovich, 1991). Furthermore, there is now a strong body of evidence suggesting that the ability to phonetically analyze novel words, or to apply phonetic cues to the identification of words in text, is one of several critical abilities that underlie the acquisition of the orthographic (or sight word) reading skills central to reading fluency (Ehri, 1998; Share, 1995). In *Teacher-Directed PALS*, students are taught to hear phonemes within words and to phonetically analyze novel words, and they practice this skill until they are fluent with increasingly difficult words.

Fluency Development

Beyond phonological and alphabetic knowledge, students must be able to read connected text with relative ease if the meaning of that text is to be accessed and if the development of mature comprehension strategies is to prosper (Chard et al., 1995; Rashotte & Torgesen, 1985; Stanovich, 1991). Early literacy instruction that integrates alphabetic knowledge into the actual act of reading meaningful text has been shown to enhance both fluency and comprehension (Chall, 1989; Vellutino, 1991). Furthermore, providing opportunities for repeated immersion in meaningful text has also been shown to enhance both fluency and comprehension (Rashotte & Torgesen, 1985; Sindelar, Monda, & O'Shea, 1990; Weinstein & Cooke, 1992). In *Teacher-Directed PALS*, students repeatedly read both decodable stories and authentic children's trade books that become increasingly more challenging across time.

Comprehension Development

Clearly, readers must recognize words fluently in order to comprehend text, but fluency alone is not sufficient for achieving deeper levels of understanding (Daneman, 1991). Competent comprehenders are strategic; they typically follow a generalizable plan when approaching texts (Flood & Lapp, 1991). The use of children's trade books has received recent attention for facilitating children's internalization of a strategic approach to processing text (Flood & Lapp, 1991): It appears that children develop a deeper understanding of concepts of print, text structures, and increased word recognition and fluency through repeated exposure to this literature (Flood & Lapp, 1991). More specifically, repeated reading of the same authentic text enables young readers to attend to different aspects of a story and, thus, to deepen their understanding (Martinez & Roser, 1985). Use of these books has been shown to facilitate children's vocabulary and syntax development, increase interest in reading, and supply models of written language for young readers/writers (Galda & Cullinan, 1991). In *Teacher-Directed PALS*, students are taught to use a strategic approach to reading storybooks, and its lessons incorporate the use of children's trade books.

As has been shown here, each of the crucial content elements identified by researchers is directly addressed in *Teacher-Directed PALS*. Importantly, these elements are not treated as isolated skills; rather, they are laid out so that they build upon each other in an integrated way. Across lessons new elements are carefully added into the mix, to allow students time to assimilate new information with known information. Over time the lessons become increasingly more complex, but because of their careful design, the lessons never become too difficult.

Research Studies

In addition to simply being consistent with what is known about teaching reading to struggling beginning readers, *Teacher-Directed PALS* has been empirically validated in two studies (Mathes & Babyak, in press; Mathes, Jorgensen, & Menehetti, 2000). In one study, the efficacy of *Teacher-Directed PALS* was studied when *Teacher-Directed PALS* was used in tandem with *First Grade PALS*. In this particular study, one third of the teachers implemented both *Teacher-Directed PALS* and *First Grade PALS*; one third implemented just *First Grade PALS*; and one third continued to teach reading in their typical fashion. Results indicated that the lowest

performing first graders who participated in both *Teacher-Directed PALS* and *First Grade PALS* made the greatest growth in reading on multiple measures of reading. Likewise, students who participated in *First Grade PALS* made greater growth than did the lowest performing readers who were only receiving typical practice (Mathes & Babyak, in press).

In a second study, *Teacher-Directed PALS* was compared to typical practice when done as a supplemental set of lessons alone (Mathes, Torgesen, & Menehetti, 2000). The results of this study indicated that *Teacher-Directed PALS*, used alone to supplement typical instruction, significantly improved the reading growth of struggling readers compared to that achieved by struggling readers who received only typical practice. Results from this study are presented graphically in Figures 1-4.

FIGURE 1

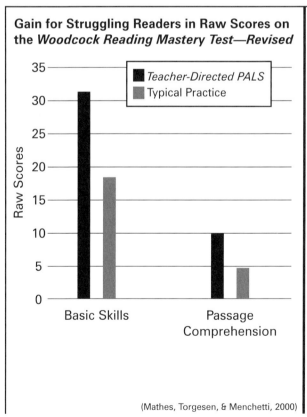

Gain for Struggling Readers in Raw Scores on the *Woodcock Reading Mastery Test—Revised*

(Mathes, Torgesen, & Menchetti, 2000)

FIGURE 2

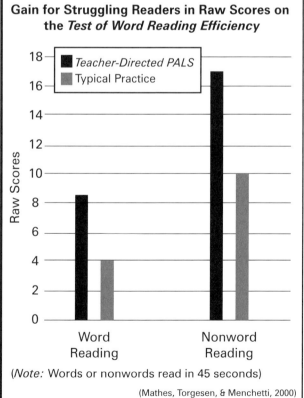

Gain for Struggling Readers in Raw Scores on the *Test of Word Reading Efficiency*

(*Note:* Words or nonwords read in 45 seconds)

(Mathes, Torgesen, & Menchetti, 2000)

FIGURE 3
FIGURE 4

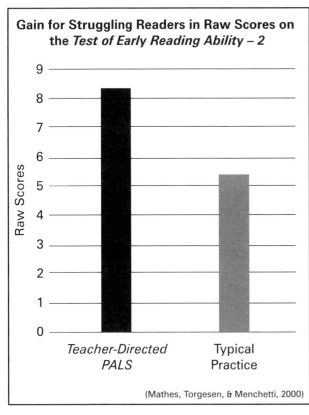

Gain for Struggling Readers in Raw Scores on the *Test of Early Reading Ability – 2*

(Mathes, Torgesen, & Menchetti, 2000)

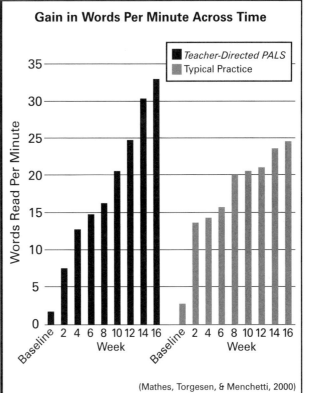

Gain in Words Per Minute Across Time

(Mathes, Torgesen, & Menchetti, 2000)

The Content

Teacher-Directed PALS teaches critical beginning reading skills in an integrated fashion. Because the program is focused only on critical content, it does not cover every phonic element or skill. Instead, it only presents elements and skills that are necessary for students to get "up and running." Thus, *Teacher-Directed PALS* should not replace a student's reading program, but instead supplement it. (The exact content presented in *Teacher-Directed PALS* is listed in the New Content Sequence section in Chapter 2.) Once students are reading, it becomes easier for them to learn additional elements presented during more traditional classroom instruction.

Within each *Teacher-Directed PALS* session, students (1) practice phonemic awareness, letter-sound recognition, and phonological decoding and apply these skills in connected text; and (2) read a trade book along with the teacher by making predictions, reading the text multiple times, and summarizing the text through retelling. Specifically, teachers and students work through two routines called Sounds and Words and Story Sharing. Sounds and Words provides for systematic, explicit instruction in synthetic phonics; Story Sharing balances the session with contextualized experiences with children's literature through the shared reading and rereading of authentic text. A short overview of each routine is presented here; each routine is covered in detail in Chapter 2 (Sounds and Words) and Chapter 3 (Story Sharing).

Sounds and Words

The first 10-20 minutes of each *Teacher-Directed PALS* session is dedicated to Sounds and Words, a set of activities designed to promote the fluent application of the alphabetic principle to connected text reading. A curriculum of 57 carefully designed daily lessons has been developed to guide teachers and students through the Sounds and Words routine. In each lesson there are several fast-paced activities: (1) Letter-Sounds, (2) Hearing Sounds, (3) Sounding Out, (4) Sight Word Reading, and (5) Passage Reading. The students work on a lesson until all members within the group can perform each of the tasks with no mistakes. Typically, students complete one lesson during each session, but sometimes achieving mastery takes more than one session. Thus, movement through the lessons is predicated on student performance rather than on days in the program. Over time, lessons become cumulatively more difficult. To ensure that you are tracking students' mastery of lesson content across time, a Mastery Monitoring Form is provided and is discussed in detail in Chapter 4.

Each Sounds and Words activity follows a simple procedure that is easy to conduct with students. In the Letter-Sounds activity, students practice immediate recognition of letter-sound correspondences or combinations of sounds presented in list form. Because many students who experience difficulty learning to read also have memory issues, Letter-Sounds is practiced twice during each session. In the second activity, Hearing Sounds, students practice phonemic segmentation of increasingly harder to segment words. The third activity, Sounding Out, teaches children to expertly use a strategy for decoding

unknown words. In the fourth activity, Sight Word Reading, students practice reading words that cannot be sounded out from sight. The Sound and Words routine culminates with Passage Reading, which provides the means for integrating and generalizing previously practiced content. Although these passages start out very simple, they cumulatively increase in difficulty until students are reading much more difficult passages.

Story Sharing

Immediately following the Sounds and Words activity, the teacher leads Story Sharing with a short book of the appropriate reading level during the time remaining (i.e., 10-15 minutes). Story Sharing was designed to teach beginning readers a strategic orientation for approaching text. There are three activities associated with Story Sharing: (1) Pretend-Read, (2) Read Aloud, and (3) Retell. All activities surround the reading of a piece of children's literature that you select (Chapter 3 provides an extensive list of ideas to help you select books). First, you quickly direct Pretend-Reading by asking students to predict what is happening on each page of the story, based on the pictures. Next, you direct Read Aloud, an echo reading activity in which you provide a fluent model of oral reading. In this activity, you and the students take turns reading each sentence of the story aloud. In the final minute of Story Sharing, you conduct Story Retell by helping the students to sequence the events of the story.

In This Manual

This manual provides all the information you need to effectively implement *Teacher-Directed PALS*. Chapter 2 provides in-depth ideas for how to conduct the Sounds and Words routine and also includes a reproducible placement test for you to use with your students. Chapter 3 offers information about conducting the Story Sharing routine, including guidelines for how to choose storybooks and an extensive list of recommended books. Chapter 4 provides suggestions and sample scripts for teaching the daily lessons; here you will also find detailed Daily Teaching Format Guides and a reproducible Mastery Monitoring Form for your use in tracking students' mastery of the concepts taught.

Following Chapter 4 are the Lesson Sheets for all 57 lessons in *Teacher-Directed PALS*.

Objectives of This Manual

After studying this manual, you will be able to:

1. Describe the benefits of teaching *Teacher-Directed PALS* lessons with beginning or struggling readers.

2. Teach alphabetic principles to students effectively, using materials from *Teacher-Directed PALS*.

3. Appropriately select and assign children's literature to be read during the *Teacher-Directed PALS* activities.

4. Use *Teacher-Directed PALS* to provide quality small group reading instruction for beginning readers.

Note: Throughout this manual the term "teacher" is used to refer to the individual who is presenting the lessons (even though this person may not be a certified teacher), and the term "student" is used to refer to the young readers who are receiving the lesson content.

CHAPTER TWO:
Sounds and Words

Objectives and Description

The Sounds and Words routine is conducted during the first 10-20 minutes of each *PALS* session and focuses on the integration of essential phonological skills to the act of reading connected text. Specific objectives for this activity are:

1. Identify letter-sound correspondences automatically.

2. Understand that words are constructed of individual sounds.

3. Blend sounds together to sound out words.

4. Recognize sight words.

5. Integrate phonological knowledge into the act of reading.

Description

Five activities initially comprise the Sounds and Words routine. Beginning with Lesson 37, the number of activities is reduced to four. Each activity appears on a daily Lesson Sheet (see Figure 5). Each activity also follows a simple procedure that is easy to conduct with students. The procedure is as follows:

1. **Letter-Sounds** (Activities 1 and 3): A series of letters is listed on the Lesson Sheet. You point to each letter and ask the students to say each sound. Students must say the sound immediately, or it is considered an error. In lessons in which a new letter-sound correspondence is to be presented, a "new sound" box appears above the list. The new sound is presented initially by the teacher and is then practiced as part of the list of letters, along with previously learned sounds. Letter-Sounds is actually done twice each day (Activities 1 and 3) during Lessons 1-36 to ensure that students are developing complete automaticity for recognizing the sound each letter represents. However, from Lesson 37 forward, students only practice Letter-Sounds one time per session.

2. **Hearing Sounds** (Activity 2): Hearing Sounds is only included in Lessons 1-36; it is omitted starting with Lesson 37. In this activity, students practice segmenting words that they hear into their component sounds or phonemes. For this activity, a series of phonologically regular words (words that can be sounded out) is listed in small type on the Lesson Sheet. You read each word aloud and the students say each sound heard by "stretching the word" and holding up one finger for each sound. (To assist the students, the number of sounds in each word is listed in parentheses under the word.) For example, *man* is stretched as /mmm/aaa/nnn/. After stretching the word, students then say the word normally again by telling what word was stretched.

3. **Sounding Out** (Activity 4): For this activity, a series of phonetically regular words appears in list form on the

Lesson Sheet; dots appear below each letter-sound correspondence in the word. The students' job is to sound out each word by saying each sound in the word as you touch the corresponding dot. The students are taught to say each sound in the word slowly, and not to stop between sounds. Once the students have sounded the word out, they read the word as a whole. (Starting at Lesson 37, students will sound out words by syllable rather than by letter. Hence, the dots are not used on Lesson Sheets 37-57; on these Sheets each syllable is underlined.)

4. **Sight Words** (Activity 5): In this activity, a group of irregular sight words is presented in list form. Students must quickly tell what each word is. In lessons in which a new sight word is presented, the new word is located in a "new word" box, which is presented initially by the teacher and then practiced as part of the list of words.

5. **Passage Reading** (Activity 6): (This activity does not begin until Lesson 36.) The skills practiced in Activities 1-5 are integrated through Passage Reading. In this activity, students read a passage comprised of words that they have all the skills to read. These passages start out very simple, but they cumulatively increase in difficulty. Students initially read the story with you controlling the reading rate by pointing to each word. Then students read the passage again, but they take over the task of pointing to each word. Students should be told to read as quickly and as smoothly as they can.

FIGURE 5A
SAMPLE GAME SHEET

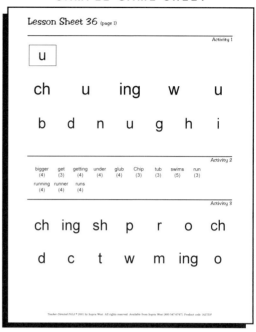

FIGURE 5B
SAMPLE GAME SHEET

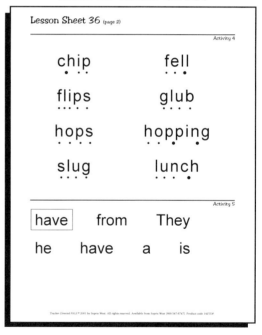

Lesson Sheet 36 (page 3)

Activity 6

Chip the bug fell in the tub. Plop! Rub a dub dub. Chip swims and bobs. He dips and flips.

Pug the slug hops into the tub with Chip. They have fun in the tub. Glub, glub, glub.

Teacher-Directed PALS © 2001 by Sopris West. All rights reserved. Available from Sopris West (800) 547-6747). Product code 142TDP.

Sounds and Words Lesson Design

A set of 57 lessons has been developed and empirically validated specifically for the Sounds and Words routine of *Teacher-Directed PALS*. Building on instructionally sound design principles (e.g., Carnine, Silbert, & Kameenui, 1997) the Lesson Sheets include the following features:

1. No more than one letter-sound correspondence or sight word is introduced in a lesson.

2. Previously mastered letter-sound correspondences and sight words are reviewed in each lesson.

3. Letter-sound correspondences and sight words of higher frequency are presented first.

4. The initial introductions of letter-sound correspondences and sight words that are auditorily and/or visually similar are kept apart.

5. Letter-sound correspondences that are to be introduced in the near future are first practiced orally by incorporating them into the Hearing Sounds activity.

6. Once introduced, letter-sound correspondences are incorporated into words to be sounded out, and then into words found in simple passages.

7. The introduction of word types is controlled for difficulty. Across time, word types become cumulatively more advanced so that students gain mastery of the sounding out strategy.

8. Introduction of a new word type to be sounded out is preceded with auditory practice of words of that type during the Hearing Sounds activity.

9. Once students have developed advanced phonemic awareness ability, that skill is no longer practiced, providing more time to focus on connected text practice.

Sounds and Words: New Content Lesson Sequence

Table 1 shows the sequence of concepts introduced in the *Teacher-Directed PALS* lessons. Blanks indicate cumulative review.

TABLE 1

Teacher-Directed PALS Sequence of Concepts

Lesson	Letter Sound Correspondence	Phonemic Awareness Concept (Hearing Sounds activity)	Word Type (Sounding Out activity) v = vowel c = consonant	Sight Word
1	a	segmenting & blending vc & cvc	vc	the
2	t			
3	s		cvc	
4				
5				
6				is
7	i	vcc		
8				
9		cvc'c		on
10	f	cvcc	cvcc	
11				
12			cvc's	was
13	d			a
14	r			
15				from
16	o			with
17	g	ccvcc		
18				
19				
20	h		ccvc	
21				
22	c		ccvcc	has
23				
24	l			
25	e			because
26				
27	n			he
28	b	cvccc		
29		ccvccc		
30	w			to
31	p	cccvc		are

TABLE 1 (continued)

Teacher-Directed PALS Sequence of Concepts

Lesson	Letter Sound Correspondence	Phonemic Awareness Concept (Hearing Sounds activity)	Word Type (Sounding Out activity) v = vowel c = consonant	Sight Word
32				
33	ing	multisyllabic words	multisyllabic words	she
34	ch			they
35				
36	u			have

(Note: Phonemic awareness removed; Passage Reading begins; Letter-Sounds is reduced to one activity per lesson.)

Lesson	Letter Sound Correspondence	Phonemic Awareness Concept (Hearing Sounds activity)	Word Type (Sounding Out activity) v = vowel c = consonant	Sight Word
37	er	Note: Hearing Sounds removed.	Note: Sounding Out is done by syllable, not by letter.	than
38				
39	j			his
40	k			of
41	ck			
42				look
43	ee			their
44	ea			
45				I
46	sh			for
47	aw			over
48			-ed (not presented directly)	
49	ur			as, when
50	ir			said
51				
52	th			your
53	ou			my, too
54				
55	ow (as in owl)			were
56	ar			
57				you

Content Not Taught in Teacher-Directed PALS

As mentioned previously, *Teacher-Directed PALS* does not teach every phonetic element and skill, focusing instead on getting students "up and going" with beginning reading. However, if students complete all 57 lessons, they will be ready to learn additional, more complex, phonics elements. We suggest that you tap into another already existing curriculum to guide additional instruction, but continue to use the teaching techniques utilized in *Teacher-Directed PALS*.

Skills that you will want to continue with include:

1. Long vowel pattern vc$_e$ (a_e, e_e, i_e, o_e, u_e).

2. More complex combination sound correspondences, such as: *ai*, *ay*, *qu*, *dge*, *tch*, *ge*, *gi*, *ce*, *ci*, *ere*, *are*, *igh*.

3. The concept that *X* represents two phonemes (/ks/) as in *ax*.

4. Derivatives of the letter *y*.

5. Variants of any one sound.

6. Phonetic irregularity within words.

Once students are already reading, they can more readily grasp this new content.

Thus, creating additional lessons to teach these new elements becomes much easier once you complete the original 57 lessons.

Pronouncing Sounds

When presenting *Teacher-Directed PALS* lessons to your students, you will be modeling how phonemes or sounds are pronounced when they are isolated from other sounds in words. You will be modeling sounds during the Letter-Sounds, Hearing Sounds, and Sounding Out activities; in each of these activities it will be very important to pronounce the sounds the way that they are actually said in words. If you distort a sound you may confuse many students.

Pronouncing the sounds of phonemes in isolation can be difficult. The goal is to pronounce them the same way they are pronounced in words, so that students can string them back together to form real words. In particular, this means being careful not to add an extra sound either on the front or the back of the intended sound. For example, the letter *r* is not pronounced /errr/, but rather /rrr/. To fully understand this, say aloud the word *run*. Now say it again, and hold on the /rrrr/. You did not say *erun*, you said *run*.

Kinds of Sounds

There are basically two kinds of sounds in *PALS*: continuous sounds and stop sounds.

Continuous Sounds

Most sounds can be said continuously without distortion. For example, /m/ can be held continuously for many seconds (/mmmmmmmmmm/) and the sound is still the same.

When pronouncing continuous sounds for students, it is easier for them if you hold onto the sound for about two seconds. Think of it as humming or stretching the sound. Holding the sound allows the students to process the sound more fully, helping them to better learn letter-sound correspondences and to sound out words more easily.

Stop Sounds

A small group of sounds in our language cannot be held or they will be distorted. These are called stop sounds because the speech sound must stop before distortion occurs. Typically, when stop sounds are distorted it is by adding a schwa or /uh/ sound to the end. For example /t/ is often pronounced /tuh/. For some students, this distortion leads to confusion when sounding out words. For example, when sounding out *dad*, many students would not recognize /duh/aaa/duh/ as dad, but have no trouble with /d/aaa/d/. Thus, it is very important to pronounce stop sounds quickly, without the distortion of adding a schwa sound.

> If you can hum it,
> then hold it;
> if you can't,
> then stop!

Sound Pronunciation Guide

Table 2 is designed to help you in pronouncing the letter-sound correspondences presented in *Teacher-Directed PALS*. The letters are written in the order of their appearance within the curriculum.

Continuous sound letters are represented by three repeats of the letter. For example, *m* is represented as /mmm/, and *s* is represented as /sss/. This shows that the sound is held or hummed for about two seconds.

Stop sounds are represented with only one occurrence of the letter. For example, *d* is represented as /d/, and *t* is represented as /t/. This shows that the sound just stops; it is said quickly and is not held.

TABLE 2

Teacher-Directed PALS Letter and Pronunciation Examples

Lesson	Letter– Pronunciation– Example	Lesson	Letter– Pronunciation– Example	Lesson	Letter– Pronunciation– Example
1	a – /aaa/ – am	25	e – /eee/ – red	43	ee – /ēēē/ – seed
2	t – /t/ (stop) – Tom	27	n – /nnn/ – net	44	ea – /eeee/ – bread
3	s – /sss/ – sat	28	b – /b/ (stop) – bat	46	sh – /shhh/ – shop
7	i – /iii/ – it	30	w – /www/ – wing	46	-ed (not taught directly)
10	f – /fff/ – fish	31	p – /p/ (stop) – pat	47	aw – /awww/ – claw
13	d – /d/ (stop) – Dad	33	ing – /iiing/ – sing	49	ur – /urrr/ – fur
14	r – /rrr/ – rat	34	ch – /ch/ (stop) – chip	50	ir – /irrr/ – bird
16	o – /ooo/ – on	36	u – /uuu/ – up	52	th – /ththth/ – that
17	g – /g/ (stop) – game	37	er – /errr/ – reader	53	ou – /ouououu/ – out
20	h – /h/ (stop) – hat	39	j – /j/ (stop) – Jack	55	ow – /owowow/ – cow
22	c – /c/ (stop) – cat	40	k – /k/ (stop) – kite	56	ar – /arrr/ – car
24	l – /lll/ – let	41	ck – /ck/ (stop) – chick		

(*Note:* All single vowels taught in *Teacher-Directed PALS* are short vowels.)

Sounds and Words Placement Test

Before beginning to use the Sounds and Words routine with your students, you will need to determine where in the sequence to begin instruction. If you are teaching small groups of students, it will be important to group them so that all the students in a particular group are entering the curriculum on the same lesson. Use the following placement test to determine where to begin instruction for each student.

You will need to make one copy of the test for each student in order to record his or her performance. The placement test should be administered to one student at a time.

Sounds and Words Placement Test

Student's Name: _____

Date: _____   Starting Lesson: _____

Part A: Letter-Sounds

Directions: **When I point to a letter, you tell me its sound.**

a   m   t   l   s   r   f   d

Errors: _____
- If 1 or 0 errors, move on to Part B of this test.
- If more than 1 error, start student on Lesson Sheet 1.

Part B: Sounding Out

Directions: (Point to the first word.) **Sound out this word, then read it.**
(Do the same with each word.)

mid   rats   did   Sam

Errors: _____
- If 0 errors, move on to Part C of this test.
- If any errors, start student on Lesson Sheet 1.

Part C: Connected Text

Directions: **Read this story out loud to me.**

Sam is a rat.

Sid is a ram.

Sam sat on Sid.

Sid is mad at Sam.

Errors: _____
- If 0 or 1 errors, start student on Lesson Sheet 16.
- If more than 1 error, start student on Lesson Sheet 1.

Teacher-Directed PALS © 2001 by Sopris West. All rights reserved. Available from Sopris West (800-547-6747). Product code 142TDP.

CHAPTER THREE:
Story Sharing

Objectives and Description

The last 10-15 minutes of each *PALS* session are spent conducting the Story Sharing routine. Story Sharing helps students to do the following:

1. Increase fluency and word recognition by orally reading a story of appropriate difficulty, with the teacher's help.

2. Increase memory skills, sequencing skills, and knowledge of basic story structure by predicting, sharing, and retelling a story.

Description

Immediately following the Sounds and Words activity, the pairs conduct Story Sharing for the remaining *PALS* time. Typically this routine is 10-15 minutes, depending on how quickly the daily Sounds and Words lesson was mastered. All Story Sharing activities surround the reading of a piece of children's literature that you select. The selection of text allows you to individualize by enabling you to choose texts according to the needs of individual students. Select a storybook text that can be read multiple times in the time allotted. (Details about how to best select storybooks for Story Sharing are discussed later in this chapter.)

There are three activities associated with Story Sharing: (1) Pretend-Read, (2) Read Aloud, and (3) Retell. As with Sounds and Words, each activity follows a simple routine:

1. **Pretend-Read**: During the first 1-2 minutes of Story Sharing, you guide students to predict what is happening on each page of the story, based on the pictures. When necessary, ask the students questions about the pictures to stimulate a reasonable prediction.

2. **Read Aloud**: The next 8-12 minutes are devoted to the reading and rereading of a short storybook. The goal is for the students to take over independent reading of the text selection. There are actually three simple steps to conducting Read Aloud. First, after reading the title and turning to the starting page, you and the students engage in "echo reading": you read a sentence of the story while sliding your finger under each word as you read it, then the students read the same sentence while you point. Second, you and the students "chorally read" the story together, meaning that you read the storybook with the students simultaneously. Third, the students take turns independently reading sentences from the story.

3. **Retell**: In the final 1-2 minutes of Story Sharing, you guide students to sequence the events of the story. For this activity, prompt the students to retell the story, asking "What did you learn first?" and then "What did you learn next?" If important information was left out, or information is provided out of order, guide the students to correct the information rather than

just providing them with the correct information.

How Story Sharing Develops Comprehension Skills

Story Sharing is designed to teach beginning readers a strategic orientation for approaching text. The underlying purpose of Pretend-Reading is to teach students to preview and think about text selections prior to the onset of actual reading. Likewise, it is an opportunity to stretch students' oral language skills while expanding their critical thinking skills.

Read Aloud also facilitates comprehension, communicating to beginning readers that rereading is an important part of the reading process. It also teaches or solidifies concepts of print such as directionality and print conventions, builds the foundational comprehension skill of restating information, and provides contextualized experiences with print.

Retell provides an opportunity for students to practice organizing information sequentially, and reinforces the importance of attending to information for later recall.

Selecting Appropriate Storybooks

Placing students in appropriate reading material is critical to the success of Story Sharing.

Each day, you will need to select one story to read during Story Sharing. It is fine if your students have read this book on previous occasions, as long as they still find the book engaging. Remember that repeated exposure to text is desirable for beginning readers. You should also check with the teacher who teaches reading to the students you work with (if you are not their only reading teacher) to see if there are specific titles that he or she would like your students to practice reading. To facilitate the text selection process, this book includes a list of assorted children's book titles (trade books only) that are appropriate for Story Sharing (see the end of this chapter).

Types of Text

In making text selections for your students, you should be aware that there are two kinds of storybooks that are appropriate for Story Sharing: decodable books and trade books. It is best if students have reading practice with both kinds of storybooks.

Decodable Books

Decodable books are designed to provide students with practice in applying phonetic skills to read sentences and stories. They are carefully written to include words that are decodable based on their ability to be sounded out. These books also include high frequency sight words. Usually, these books list on the front or back cover the phonetic elements and sight words that are practiced in the story. Many reading programs used for teaching reading in the general education classroom include decodable books to reinforce phonetic elements that are being taught. If the reading series being used in your students' normal reading program includes decodable text, you should also include these books in your tutoring.

Trade Books

Trade books are written to communicate a children's story without being constrained by choosing words to conform to specific phonetic elements. Typically, these books have a richer vocabulary and more fully developed story than decodable books. They often have predictable features, such as a repetitive phrase and well-designed artwork, that help young readers to identify unknown words without sounding them out. To assist you in identifying appropriate trade books for use with the students you are teaching, use the following guidelines. A detailed list of children's trade books arranged by difficulty level also follows. Begin Story Sharing with the easier levels and move students into more difficult books as they demonstrate greater text reading skill.

Guidelines for selecting trade storybooks for Story Sharing:

1. Stories must be short enough for you and the students to read and reread three times in 8-12 minutes.

2. It is important to select stories that do not extend beyond the students' memory abilities. For very low performing readers, this will need to be a very short book with few words on each page.

3. Books with which the students are already familiar can facilitate reading independently and expand students' story comprehension. Thus, using stories that the students are also reading as part of their normal reading program is desirable.

4. Stories should increase in length and difficulty as students gain more reading skill over time.

Recommended Trade Books for Use During Story Sharing

The following list is divided into sections according to difficulty/reading level. All books in this list are picture books; the list includes easiest picture books and books with one, two, or three lines or sentences per page. The annotations provide information about predictable features and text length, as well as about difficult words and multicultural considerations when applicable.

Easiest-to-Read Picture Books

Aruego, J., and A. Dewey. 1979. *We hide, you seek*. New York: Greenwillow.
Brief, simple text; many wordless pages.

Baker, K. 1991. *Hide and snake*. San Diego, CA: Harcourt Brace Jovanovich.
Simple, rhyming text; close text-picture match.

Baker, K. 1994. *Big fat hen*. San Diego, CA: Harcourt Brace Jovanovich.
Familiar rhyme.

Bang, M. 1983. *Ten, nine, eight*. New York: Greenwillow.
Counting story; African-American characters.

Bang, M. 1991. *Yellow ball*. New York: Morrow.
Limited text; rhythmic language; close text-picture match.

Barton, B. 1987. *Machines at work*. New York: Crowell.
Simple text.

Bonsall, C. 1972. *The day I had to play with my sister*. New York: Harper and Row.
An early "I Can Read" book. Simple, illustrated text with repetitive language.

Bonsall, C. 1973. *Mine's the best*. New York: HarperCollins.
An early "I Can Read" book. Simple, illustrated text with repetitive language.

Bonsall, C. 1974. *And I mean it, Stanley*. New York: HarperCollins.
An early "I Can Read" book. Simple, illustrated text with repetitive language.

Bright, R. 1959. *My red umbrella*. New York: Morrow.
Simple text with some counting. Print is small.

Browne, A. 1979. *Bear hunt*. New York: Doubleday/Bantam.
Close text-picture match.

Carle, E. 1987. *Have you seen my cat?* Saxonville, MA: Picture Book Studio.
Predictable language pattern; question-answer format; simple, limited text.

Casey, P. 1988. *Quack quack*. New York: Lothrop, Lee, and Shepard.
Simple text.

Crews, D. 1984. *School bus*. New York: Greenwillow.
Simple text; close text-picture match. Multicultural illustrations; African-American author.

Dabcovich, L. 1982. *Sleepy bear*. New York: Dutton.
Simple text; close text-picture match.

Deming, A. G. 1988. *Who is tapping at my window?* New York: Dutton.
Repetitive, rhyming language; close text-picture match.

Ernst, L. C. 1986. *Up to ten and down again*. New York: Lothrop, Lee, and Shepard.
Familiar sequence (counting).

Farjeon, E. 1990. *Cats sleep anywhere*. Philadelphia: Lippincott.
Simple, rhyming poem.

Florian, D. 1983. *People working*. New York: Crowell.
Simple text with repeated language.

Florian, D. 1989. *A year in the country*. New York: Greenwillow.
Familiar sequence (months of the year).

Florian, D. 1989. *Nature walk*. New York: Greenwillow.
Simple, rhyming text; close text-picture match.

Florian, D. 1990. *A beach day*. New York: Greenwillow.
Simple, rhyming text; close text-picture match.

Florian, D. 1990. *City street*. New York: Greenwillow.
Simple, rhyming text; close text-picture match.

Florian, D. 1992. *At the zoo*. New York: Greenwillow.
Simple, rhyming text; close text-picture match.

Gardner, B. 1985. *Guess what?* New York: Lothrop, Lee, and Shepard.
Identification book of animals; close text-picture match; good for predicting story events at page turns.

Geisert, A. 1991. *Oink*. Boston: Houghton Mifflin.
One word, *oink*, is repeated throughout the book. The pictures tell the story.

Geisert, A. 1993. *Oink oink*. Boston: Houghton Mifflin.
One word, *oink*, is repeated throughout the book. The pictures tell the story.

Ginsburg, M. 1972. *The chick and the duckling*. New York: Macmillan.
Repetitive language pattern.

Ginsburg, M. 1982. *Across the stream*. New York: Greenwillow.
Predictable, rhyming text.

Goffin, J. 1993. *Yes*. New York: Lothrop, Lee, and Shepard.
Very simple, brief text; only two words in the whole story: *no* and *yes*.

Gomi, T. 1977. *Where's the fish?* New York: Morrow.
Simple text with repetitive language; question-answer format. Japanese author.

Gomi, T. 1990. *My friends*. San Francisco: Chronicle.
Repeated language patterns; close text-picture match. Japanese author.

Gomi, T. 1991. *Who hid it?* Brookfield, CT: Millbrook.
Simple questions invite participation (a search for familiar objects hidden in the illustrations). Japanese author.

Grejniec, M. 1992. *What do you like?* New York: North-South.
Simple text; repetitive language patterns. Polish author.

Grejniec, M. 1993. *Good morning, good night*. New York: North-South.
Predictable language; concept of opposites. Polish author.

Halpern, S. 1992. *My river*. New York: Macmillan.
Repeated language.

Hawkins, C., and J. Hawkins, 1983. *Boo! Who?* Austin, TX: Holt, Rinehart, and Winston.
Rhyming text.

Hill, E. 1980. *Where's Spot?* New York: Putnam.
Simple text and story. Predictable language pattern; question-answer format.

Hoban, T. 1972. *Push-pull empty-full: A book of opposites*. New York: Macmillan.
A concept book about opposites; close text-photo match.

Hoban, T. 1974. *Where is it?* New York: Macmillan.
Simple, rhyming text.

Hutchins, P. 1971. *Rosie's walk*. New York: Aladdin.
Predictable plot; simple text.

Hutchins, P. 1982. *1 hunter*. New York: Greenwillow.
Familiar sequence (counting); close text-picture match.

Hutchins, P. 1993. *My best friend*. New York: Greenwillow.
Repetitive language; close text-picture match. African-American characters.

Jonas, A. 1986. *Now we can go*. New York: Greenwillow.
Simple text with close text-picture match.

Kalan, R. 1979. *Blue sea*. New York: Greenwillow.
Concept book about relative size; repetitive language patterns.

Keats, E. J. 1973. *Pssst! Doggie*. Danbury, CT: Franklin Watts.
Largely wordless book—only three pages have text on them.

Keats, E. J. 1973. *Skate!* Danbury, CT: Franklin Watts.
Simple text with few words.

Kraus, R. 1970. *Whose mouse are you?* New York: Macmillan.
Predictable language pattern.

Kraus, R. 1986. *Where are you going, little mouse?*. New York: Greenwillow.
Predictable language pattern; question-answer format.

Lankford, M. D. 1991. *Is it dark? Is it light?* New York: Knopf.
Predictable, repetitive language; question-answer format. Last page has the word moon in many languages.

Leedy, L. 1987. *Big, small, short, tall*. New York: Holiday House.
A concept book about opposites; close text-picture match.

MacDonald, S. 1986. *Alphabatics*. New York: Aladdin.
ABC book.

Martin, B., Jr. 1983. *Brown bear, brown bear, what do you see?* New York: Holt.
Repetitive language pattern; question-answer format.

McDonnell, F. 1994. *I love animals.* Cambridge, MA: Candlewick.
Simple text with repeated phrase throughout.

McMillan, B. 1983. *Here a chick, there a chick*. New York: Lothrop, Lee, and Shepard.
A photographic concept book about opposites; close text-photograph match.

McMillan, B. 1984. *Kitten can. . . .* New York: Lothrop, Lee, and Shepard.
A photographic concept book about verbs; close text-photograph match.

McMillan, B. 1988. *Growing colors*. New York: Lothrop, Lee, and Shepard.
A photographic concept book about colors.

McMillan, B. 1989. *Super, super, superwords*. New York: Lothrop, Lee, and Shepard.
A concept book about comparative adjectives. Contains multicultural photographs.

McMillan, B. 1991. *One, two, one pair!* New York: Scholastic.
A concept book about pairs. Only three words appear throughout the text (the words in the title).

McMillan, B. 1992. *Beach ball-left, right*. New York: Holiday House.
A concept book about *left* and *right*. Only two words appear on each two-page spread of the book: *left* and *right*.

McMillan, B. 1993. *Mouse views: What the class pet saw*. New York: Holiday House.
A photographic visual perception concept story; good for predicting story events at page turns.

Micklethwait, L. 1992. *I spy: An alphabet in art*. New York: Greenwillow.
ABC book. The illustrations are famous paintings with objects from A to Z to "spy."

Miller, M. 1990. *Who uses this?* New York: Greenwillow.
Question-answer format; one question is repeated throughout the book. Contains multicultural photographs.

Norworth, J. 1993. *Take me out to the ballgame*. Salem, OR: Four Winds.
Familiar song; brief, rhyming text.

Omerod, J. 1992. *Come back, kittens*. New York: Lothrop, Lee, and Shepard.
Repetitive language pattern.

Omerod, J. 1992. *Come back, puppies*. New York: Lothrop, Lee, and Shepard.
Repetitive language pattern.

Paterson, B. 1989. *My first wild animals*. New York: HarperCollins.
Animal identification book.

Pomerantz, C. 1984. *Where's the bear?* New York: Greenwillow.
Predictable, repetitive, very simple text.

Raffi. 1988. *One light, one sun*. New York: Crown.
Repetitive language.

Raffi. 1988. *Wheels on the bus*. New York: Crown.
Familiar song/rhyme. Predictable, repetitive language patterns.

Raffi. 1989. *Five little ducks*. New York: Crown.
Familiar song/rhyme and familiar sequence (counting); repetitive language pattern.

Raschka, C. 1993. *Yo! Yes?* Danbury, CT: Jackson/Orchard Books/Watts.
Close text-picture match; interracial friendship.

Rees, M. 1988. *Ten in a bed*. Boston: Little/Joy Street.
Familiar sequence (counting); repetitive language pattern.

Rikys, B. 1992. *Red bear*. New York: Dial.
A concept book about colors; very simple story with good picture cues.

Rockwell, A. 1980. *Honk honk!* New York: Dutton.
Repetitive language patterns; cumulative story.

Rose, A. 1992. *Hide and seek in the yellow house*. New York: Viking.
Simple, repetitive text.

Samton, S. W. 1991. *Moon to sun: An adding book*. Honesdale, PA: Caroline House.
Familiar sequence (counting); concept book about simple addition, with cumulative language patterns. Close text-picture match.

Samton, S. W. 1991. *On the river: an adding book*. Honesdale, PA: Caroline House.
Familiar sequence (counting); concept book about simple addition, with cumulative language patterns. Close text-picture match.

Serfozo, M. 1988. *Who said red?* New York: McElderry.
Repetitive language pattern; question-answer format.

Shaw, C. G. 1947. *It looked like spilt milk*. New York: HarperCollins.
Repetitive language patterns; good picture cues.

Shannon, D. 1999. *No, David!* New York: Blue Sky Press.
Simple text with vivid pictures.

Stott, D. 1990. *Too much*. New York: Dutton.
Simple text.

Stott, D. 1991. *Little duck's bicycle ride*. New York: Dutton.
Simple text.

Stott, D. 1993. *Kitty and me*. New York: Dutton.
Simple, brief text.

Stott, D. 1993. *Puppy and me*. New York: Dutton.
Simple, brief text.

Suen, A. 1998. *Window music*. New York: Viking.
Rhyming language.

Tafuri, N. 1986. *Have you seen my duckling?* New York: Puffin.
Predictable language pattern; very simple, limited text with many wordless pages. One question repeated throughout the text.

Tafuri, N. 1986. *Who's counting?* New York: Grecnwillow.
Familiar sequence (counting); close text-picture match.

Tafuri, N. 1988. *Spots, feathers, and curly tails*. New York: Greenwillow.
Predictable question-answer format with repetitive language; very simple text with large print.

Tafuri, N. 1994. *This is the farmer*. New York: Greenwillow.
Very simple text with large print.

Titherington, J. 1986. *Pumpkin pumpkin*. New York: Mulberry.
Repetitive language patterns.

Wagner, K. 1990. *Chocolate chip cookies*. New York: Holt.
Presents cookie baking sequence.

Wellington, M. 1992. *The sheep follow*. New York: Dutton.
Repetitive language pattern.

Wheeler, C. 1982. *Marmalade's yellow leaf*. New York: Knopf.
Simple, brief text.

Williams, S. 1990. *I went walking*. New York: Gulliver/Harcourt Brace Jovanovich.
Question-answer format; repetitive, rhyming language pattern.

Wolcott, P. 1991. *The marvelous mud washing machine*. New York: Random House.
"A 10-Word Reader." Repetitive language.

Wood, R. 1982. *What's next?* Boston: Houghton Mifflin.
Question-answer format; one repeated question throughout.

Wood, D., and A. Wood. 1992. *Piggies*. San Diego, CA: Harcourt Brace Jovanovich.
Repetitive language pattern.

Yektai, N. 1984. *Sun rain*. Salem, OR: Four Winds.
Very simple text with good picture cues.

Yektai, N. 1987. *Bears in pairs*. New York: Bradbury Press.
Simple, rhyming, repetitive text. Close text-picture match.

Yektai, N. 1990. *Hi bears, bye bears*. Danbury, CT: Orchard.
Rhyming text with repetitive language. Close text-picture match.

Zinnemann-Hope, P. 1986. *Let's go shopping, Ned*. New York: McElderry.
Some rhyming words.

Zinnemann-Hope, P. 1986. *Time for bed, Ned*. New York: McElderry.
Some rhyming words.

Zinnemann-Hope, P. 1987. *Find your coat, Ned*. New York: McElderry.
Some rhyming words.

Zinnemann-Hope, P. 1987. *Let's play ball, Ned*. New York: McElderry.
Some rhyming words.

Picture Books With One Sentence or One Line per Page

Aliki. 1996. *Go tell Aunt Rhody*. New York: Aladdin.
Familiar song/rhyme; repetitive language pattern.

Anholt, C. 1990. *Good days, bad days*. New York: G. P. Putnam's Sons.
Repetitive, brief text. One phrase/line per page; first page has four short lines.

Baker, K. 1990. *Who is the beast?* San Diego, CA: Harcourt Brace Jovanovich.
Rhyming, predictable text.

Barrett, J. 1983. *What's left?* New York: Atheneum.
Predictable question-answer format.

Barton, B. 1982. *Airport*. New York: HarperCollins.

Barton, B. 1986. *Airplanes*. New York: Crowell.
Simple text.

Barton, B. 1986. *Trains*. New York: Crowell.
Brief text with a few difficult words (*electric, freight, passengers*).

Barton, B. 1986. *Trucks*. New York: Crowell.
Brief text with a few difficult words (*cement, delivering, hauling*).

Barton, B. 1989. *Dinosaurs, dinosaurs*. New York: Crowell.
Brief, simple text.

Barton, B. (1990). *Bones, bones, dinosaur bones*. New York: Crowell.
Rhythmic language. Second page has a list of difficult dinosaur names; the rest of the text is easy to read. Most pages have one line.

Barton, B. 1992. *I want to be an astronaut*. New York: HarperCollins.
Brief text with a few difficult words (*gravity, mission*).

Beller, J. 1984. *A-B-C-ing: An action alphabet*. New York: Crown.
Familiar sequence (alphabet). Photographs provide text cues; children of different races are shown. One word per page.

Brown, C. 1991. *My barn*. New York: Greenwillow/Morrow.
Repetitive language pattern; students will enjoy reading and making the animal sounds on each page. One sentence with two or three lines per page.

Brown, R. 1981. *A dark, dark tale*. New York: Dial.
Repetitive language pattern. One sentence with two lines per page.

Bucknall, C. 1985. *One bear all alone*. New York: Dial.
Familiar sequence (counting); rhyming text. One sentence per page; last page has two sentences.

Buller, J., and S. Schade. 1988. *I love you, goodnight*. New York: Simon and Schuster.
Repetitive, rhyming, predictable text. Close text-picture match.

Burgess, M. 1991. *One little teddy bear*. New York: Viking.
Familiar sequence (counting); rhyming text. One sentence with four lines per page.

Burningham, J. 1978. *Time to get out of the bath, Shirley*. New York: Crowell.

Burton, M. R. 1986. *Oliver's birthday*. New York: Harper and Row.
Predictable, repeated words.

Butler, D. 1991. *Higgledy piggledy hobbledy hoy*. New York: Greenwillow.
Rhyming text with repetitive language. Some difficult nonsense words.

Carroll, K. S. 1992. *One red rooster*. Boston: Houghton Mifflin.
Familiar sequence (counting); rhyming language.

Chapman, C. 1993. *Pass the fritters, critters*. Salem, OR: Four Winds.
Rhyming words.

Cherry, L. 1988. *Who's sick today?* New York: Dutton.
Rhyming language patterns; a few difficult animal names (*gnu, llamas, stoats*). One phrase or sentence on one line per page; last page has two sentences.

Christelow, E. 1989. *Five little monkeys jumping on the bed*. New York: Clarion.
Familiar sequence (counting); repetitive, rhyming text. One or two sentences on one line per page.

Crews, D. 1981. *Light*. New York: Greenwillow.
Very brief text with repeated words. African-American author. One word or phrase on one line per page.

Crews, D. 1982. *Carousel*. New York: Greenwillow.
Simple, brief text; a few difficult words (*blaring, calliope, saddled*). African-American author. One short phrase or sentence per page.

Crews, D. 1986. *Ten black dots*. New York: William Morrow.
Familiar sequence (counting); rhyming text. African-American author. One phrase per page; last page has three sentences.

Domanska, J., ed. 1985. *Busy Monday morning*. New York: Greenwillow.
Repetitive text; familiar sequence (days of the week).

Driscoll, D. 1994. *Three two one day*. New York: Simon and Schuster.
Familiar sequence (days of the week); rhyming text with close text-picture match. A few difficult words (*bruise, cinnamon, explore*). Most pages have one sentence on two lines.

Duke, K. 1983. *The guinea pig ABC*. New York: Dutton.
ABC book. Close text-picture match; some difficult words. One word per page.

Ehlert, L. 1987. *Growing vegetable soup*. San Diego, CA: Harcourt Brace Jovanovich.
Familiar sequence. One sentence or less (one to four short lines) per page.

Ehlert, L. 1990. *Feathers for lunch*. San Diego, CA: Harcourt Brace Jovanovich.
Rhyming text.

Evans, K. 1994. *Hunky dory found it*. New York: Dutton.
Predictable, repetitive language pattern. One sentence per page; one page has two sentences.

Emberly, E. 1992. *Go away, big green monster!* New York: Little, Brown.
Repetitive language pattern.

Fleming, D. 1992. *Count!* New York: Holt.
Familiar sequence (counting); some difficult words (*gnu, quiet, toucan*).

Fleming, D. 1992. *In the tall, tall grass.* New York: Holt.
Rhyming text. Two to five words in large print per page.

Fleming, D. 1992. *Lunch.* New York: Holt.
Predictable text due to illustrations; simple plot; good for predicting story events at page turns.

Fleming, D. 1993. *In the small, small pond.* New York: Holt.
Rhyming text. Three or four words in large print per page.

Florian, D. 1991. *Vegetable garden.* San Diego, CA: Harcourt Brace Jovanovich.
Brief, rhyming text; some difficult words (*cauliflower, cucumber, harvest, seedlings, sprout*).

Fox, M. 1993. *Time for bed.* New York: Gulliver/Harcourt Brace Jovanovich.
Predictable, repetitive language pattern. One sentence on two lines per page.

Goennel, H. 1986. *Seasons.* New York: Little, Brown.
Familiar sequence (seasons of the year); repetitive language patterns. Most pages have one phrase or sentence; first page has four short sentences and last page has two sentences.

Goennel, H. 1988. *My day.* New York: Little, Brown.
One phrase or sentence on one line per page; first page has two sentences.

Goennel, H. 1989. *If I were a penguin. . . .* New York: Little, Brown.
Repeated phrase throughout. One phrase or sentence on one line per page; first page has two sentences.

Goennel, H. 1989. *My dog.* Danbury, CT: Orchard.
Repeated phrase throughout; some difficult words (names of dogs, e.g., *chihuahua, cocker spaniel, labrador*). One sentence on one or two lines per page.

Goennel, H. 1990. *Colors.* New York: Little, Brown.
One sentence on one line per page, first page has three sentences.

Gomi, T. 1984. *First comes Harry.* New York: Morrow.
Repeated phrase throughout. Japanese author. One line per page; one page has three lines.

Grejniec, M. 1990. *When I open my eyes.* New York: Holt.
Repetitive language patterns. Polish author. One phrase or sentence per page; last page has three sentences.

Gwynne, F. 1970. *The king who rained.* New York: Simon and Schuster.
Features homonyms; close text-picture match. One sentence on one to three lines per page.

Hale, S. J. 1990. *Mary had a little lamb.* New York: Scholastic.
Familiar rhyme. Features an African-American "Mary" character. A few difficult words (*eager, linger, patiently, appear*).

Halpern, S. 1993. *Moving from one to ten.* New York: Macmillan.
Familiar sequence (counting).

Hawkins, C., and J. Hawkins. 1983. *Pat the cat.* New York: G. P. Putnam's Sons.
Rhyming text. One sentence on one or two lines per page; one page has two sentences.

Hawkins, C., and J. Hawkins. 1984. *Mig the pig*. New York: G. P. Putnam's Sons.
Rhyming text. One sentence on one to three lines per page.

Hawkins, C., and J. Hawkins. 1985. *Jen the hen*. New York: G. P. Putnam's Sons.
Rhyming text. One sentence on one to four lines per page.

Hawkins, C., and J. Hawkins. 1988. *Zug the bug*. New York: G. P. Putnam's Sons.
Rhyming text. One sentence or less on one to three lines per page; one page has two sentences.

Heller, N. 1992. *Up the wall*. New York: Greenwillow.
Most pages have one phrase or sentence; one page has two sentences.

Hoban, T. 1979. *One little kitten*. New York: Greenwillow.
Rhyming language pattern. Close text-photograph match.

Hoff, S. 1960. *Who will be my friends?* New York: Harper and Row.
An early "I Can Read" book. Simple, illustrated text with repetitive language patterns. One sentence per page; the last two pages each have two sentences.

Hoguet, S. R. 1986. *Solomon Grundy*. New York: Dutton.
Familiar rhyme; familiar sequence (days of the week). A few difficult words (*christened, married*).

Howard, J. R. 1985. *When I'm sleepy*. New York: Dutton.
Repeated phrase throughout; a few difficult words (*downy, ledge*). Most pages have one line; the last page has three lines.

Hutchins, P. 1971. *Titch*. New York: Macmillan.
Familiar sequence. One to three lines with one sentence or less per page.

Hutchins, P. 1983. *You'll soon grow into them, Titch*. New York: Mulberry.
Repetitive language patterns.

Inkpen, M. 1987. *One bear at bedtime*. New York: Little, Brown.
Familiar sequence (counting); close text-picture match (watch for the nine caterpillars throughout the book). One phrase/sentence on one to four short lines per page.

Isadora, R. 1983. *City seen from A to Z*. New York: Greenwillow.
ABC book with multicultural characters; African-American author. One or two words per page.

Joyce, W. 1991. *George shrinks*. New York: HarperCollins.
Close text-picture match. First page has a three-line sentence; the rest of the pages have one line per page.

Kasza, K. 1990. *When the elephant walks*. New York: G. P. Putnam's Sons.
Repetitive language patterns. One phrase or sentence per page; one page has two sentences.

Keats, E. J. 1974. *Kitten for a day*. New York: Four Winds/Macmillan.
Brief text.

Keller, H. 1983. *Ten sleepy sheep*. New York: Greenwillow.
Familiar sequence (counting); predictable language. Most pages have one sentence or less on one to four lines.

Koch, M. 1989. *Just one more*. New York: Greenwillow.
Singular and plural noun pairs; close text-picture match. One word per page.

Koch, M. 1991. *Hoot howl hiss*. New York: Greenwillow/Morrow.
Predictable language pattern; close text-picture match. A few difficult words (*bleat, mountain, screech, whistle*).

Koontz, R. M. 1988. *This old man: The counting song*. New York: Dodd, Mead.
Familiar counting rhyme; repetitive language pattern.

Krauss, R. 1945. *The carrot seed*. New York: Harper and Row.
Simple text with repetitive language.

Krauss, R. 1987. *Big and little*. New York: Scholastic.
Repetitive language pattern; brief text.

Langner, N. 1969. *Miss Lucy*. New York: Macmillan.
Rhyming, repetitive language pattern.

Leedy, L. 1985. *A number of dragons*. New York: Holiday House.
Familiar sequence (counting). Rhyming text. One phrase or sentence on one or two lines per page.

Lenski, L. 1965. *Sing a song of people*. New York: Little, Brown.
Simple, rhyming text; city setting. One phrase or sentence on one or two lines per page.

Lillie, P. 1991. *When the rooster crowed*. New York: Greenwillow.
Repetitive language pattern. One phrase/sentence on one or two lines per page.

Lillie, P. 1993. *When this box is full*. New York: Greenwillow.
Familiar sequence (months of the year); repetitive, cumulative language. Close text-picture match. African-American characters and illustrator. Most pages have one phrase; there is also a growing list of the months of the year.

Maris, R. 1985. *Is anyone home?* New York: Greenwillow.
Simple text with repetitive language. One short sentence on one to two lines per page.

Maris, R. 1987. *In my garden*. New York: Greenwillow.
Familiar sequence (counting); rhyming language.

Maris, R. 1989. *Bernard's boring day*. New York: Delacorte.
Repeated language pattern.

Martin, B., Jr. 1991. *Polar bear, polar bear, what do you hear?* New York: Holt.
Repetitive language pattern; question-answer format. Some difficult words.

Martin, B., Jr., and J. Archambault. 1988. *Listen to the rain*. New York: Holt.
Rhythmic, melodic text; some difficult words. One phrase on one to five short lines per page.

Mayer, M. 1968. *There's a nightmare in my closet*. New York: Dial/Penguin.
Close text-picture match. One sentence on one to two lines per page.

Mayer, M. 1973. *Bubble bubble*. Roxbury, CT: Rainbird.
Repeated language pattern; a few difficult words.

McCarthy, B. 1992. *Ten little hippos*. New York: Bradbury.
Familiar sequence (counting); rhyming text.

Merriam, E. 1988. *Train leaves the station*. New York: Holt.
Rhyming poem with a familiar sequence (counting). One phrase or sentence on one or two lines per page.

Neumeier, M., and B. Glaser. 1984. *Action alphabet*. New York: Greenwillow.
ABC book. Close text-picture match. One word per page.

Noll, S. 1990. *Watch where you go*. New York: Greenwillow.

Polushkin, M. 1983. *Morning*. Salem, OR: Four Winds.
Repeated language.

Raffi. 1987. *Down by the bay: Songs to read*. New York: Crown.
Repetitive, rhyming song. One sentence on one to four lines per page.

Rehm, K., and K. Koike. 1991. *Left or right?* New York: Clarion.
A concept book about left and right. Question-answer format with a repetitive question pattern. Most pages have one phrase or sentence on one or two lines.

Rockwell, A. 1982. *Boats*. New York: Dutton.

Rockwell, A. 1984. *Cars*. New York: Dutton.

Rockwell, A. 1985. *Planes*. New York: Dutton.

Rockwell, A. 1986. *Big wheels*. New York: Dutton.

Rockwell, A. 1986. *Fire engines*. New York: Dutton.

Rose, R. 1986. *The cake that Mack ate*. Boston: Joy Street/Little, Brown.
Cumulative tale with repeated phrases. One sentence on one to eight lines per page.

Rossetti, C. 1992. *Color*. New York: HarperCollins.
Rhyming text about colors; question-answer format.

Scott, A. H. 1990. *One good horse: A cowpuncher's counting book*. New York: Greenwillow.
Familiar sequence (counting); a few difficult words (*buckaroos, cedar, quail*).

Sis, P. 1989. *Going up!* New York: Greenwillow.
Familiar sequence (counting); close text-picture match. A few difficult words (*astronaut, costume, surgeon*).

Spier, P. 1972. *Fast-slow, high-low: A book of opposites*. New York: Doubleday.
A concept book about opposites; close text-picture match. Two to four words per page.

Stadler, J. 1984. *Hooray for Snail!* New York: Harper and Row.

Taylor, J. 1987. *My cat*. New York: Macmillan.

Wallwork, A. 1993. *No dodos: A counting book of endangered animals*. New York: Scholastic.
Familiar sequence (counting); close text-picture match. Detailed information about the featured endangered animals is provided at the end of the book.

Ward, C. 1988. *Cookie's week*. New York: Putnam.
Predictable story; familiar sequence (days of the week).

Weiss, N. 1989. *Dog boy cap skate*. New York: Greenwillow.
Brief, rhyming text. One or two words per page.

Wellington, M. 1989. *All my little ducklings*. New York: Dutton.
Features language play, with a few difficult words. One to three phrases per page.

West, C. 1986. *Have you seen the crocodile?* Philadelphia, PA: Lippincott.
Predictable, repetitive language patterns; cumulative tale.

Westcott, N. B. 1988. *The lady with the alligator purse*. New York: Little, Brown.
Predictable language pattern; familiar rhyme. Some difficult words. Most pages have one phrase or sentence on one to four lines.

Wheeler, C. 1985. *Rose*. New York: Knopf.

Wildsmith, B. 1980. *Animal tricks*. New York: Oxford.
Rhyming text; a few difficult words (*balance, quite*).

Williams, G. 1946. *The chicken book*. New York: Delacorte.
Rhyming text.

Winter, S. 1993. *I can*. New York: Dorling Kindersley.
Simple text; repetitive language patterns.

Winter, S. 1993. *Me too*. New York: Dorling Kindersley.
Simple text; repetitive language patterns.

Winthrop, E. 1986. *Shoes*. New York: Harper and Row.
Rhyming text; a few difficult words (*blister, especially, raise*). Most pages have one line; two pages have four lines each.

Wolff, A. 1986. *A year of beasts*. New York: Dutton.
Familiar sequence (months of the year). First page has a seven-line sentence; the rest of the pages have one line per page.

Wood, A. 1992. *Silly Sally*. San Diego, CA: Harcourt Brace Jovanovich.
Rhyming text; predictable, repetitive language pattern. One phrase or sentence on one or two lines per page.

Wood, J. 1990. *One bear with bees in his hair*. New York: Dutton.
Familiar sequence (counting); rhyming text. One line (one or two short sentences) per page.

Yaccarino, D. 1993. *Big brother Mike*. Winnipeg, Canada: Hyperion.
A few difficult words.

Yektai, N. 1987. *What's missing?* New York: Clarion.
Repetitive language; question-answer format. Close text-picture match.

Yektai, N. 1989. *What's silly?* New York: Clarion.
Repetitive language; question-answer format. Close text-picture match.

Young, R. 1992. *Golden bear*. New York: Viking.
Rhyming text; African-American characters. Some difficult words. One or two phrases/lines per page.

Zuromskis, D. S. 1978. *The farmer in the dell*. New York: Little, Brown.
Familiar rhyme; repetitive language. One sentence or less on one to four lines per page.

Picture Books With up to Two Sentences or Two Lines per Page

Axworthy, A. 1993. *Along came Toto*. Cambridge, MA: Candlewick.
Predictable, repetitive language pattern. One or two sentences/lines per page; one page has four sentences.

Barrett, J. 1986. *Pickles have pimples and other silly statements*. New York: Atheneum.
Predictable, rhyming text; close text-picture match.

Bernhard, D. 1992. *What's Maggie up to?* New York: Holiday House.
A few difficult words.

Bridwell, N. 1963. *Clifford the big red dog*. New York: Scholastic.
One or two sentences per page; one page has three sentences.

Brown, M. W. 1947. *Goodnight moon*. New York: Harper and Row.
Predictable plot; simple text.

Brown, M. W. 1956. *Big red barn*. New York: Harper and Row.
Rhyming language. Most pages have one or two sentences; a few pages have three sentences.

Burningham, J. 1977. *Come away from the water, Shirley*. New York: Crowell.

Butler, D. 1988. *My brown bear Barney*. New York: Greenwillow.
Predictable, repetitive language patterns; good picture cues. Some difficult words.

Carle, E. 1984. *The very busy spider*. New York: Philomel.
Predictable, repetitive language pattern. First and last pages have three to five sentences; the rest of the pages have two sentences (one line) per page.

Carle, E. 1997. *From head to toe*. New York: HarperCollins.
Predictable, repetitive language patterns. Invites participation.

Cowen-Fletcher, J. 1993. *Mama zooms*. New York: Scholastic.
Repeated phrase throughout; features a mother in a wheelchair.

Crews, D. 1978. *Freight train*. New York: Mulberry.
Familiar concept (colors). African-American author.

Crews, D. 1998. *Night at the fair*. New York: Greenwillow.
Vivid illustrations. African-American author. One or two brief sentences per page; one page has four sentences.

Dabcovich, L. 1988. *Busy beavers*. New York: Dutton.

Domanska, J. 1974. *What do you see?* New York: Macmillan.
Rhyming text.

Evans, K. 1992. *Hunky dory ate it*. New York: Dutton.
Repetitive, rhyming text. One or two sentences on one to four lines per page.

Everitt, B. 1992. *Mean soup*. San Diego, CA: Harcourt Brace Jovanovich.

Florian, D. 1989. *Turtle day*. New York: Crowell.
Predictable, repetitive language.

Galdone, P. 1984. *The teeny-tiny woman: A ghost story*. New York: Clarion/Ticknor & Fields.
Repetitive language pattern. One or two sentences on one to seven lines per page.

Galdone, P. 1986. *Three little kittens*. New York: Clarion.
Mother Goose rhyme; repetitive language pattern.

Gammell, S. 1981. *Once upon MacDonald's farm. . . .* Salem, OR: Four Winds.
One or two sentences on one to three lines per page.

Gardner, B. 1987. *Can you imagine. . .? A counting book*. New York: G. P. Putnam's Sons.
Familiar sequence (counting); rhyming text. Some difficult words (*armadillos, photographs, twirling, veils*).

Garne, S. T. 1992. *One white sail*. New York: Green Tiger/Simon.
Counting book; rhythmic, rhyming text; story set in the Caribbean. Some difficult words (*tune, trail, neath, island*).

Ginsburg, M. 1973. *Three kittens*. New York: Crown.
Predictable plot; repetitive language pattern.

Goennel, H. 1992. *It's my birthday*. New York: Tambourine.
A few difficult words (*magician, pirates, treasure*). One or two sentences on one to three lines per page; last page has three sentences.

Goode, D. 1988. *I hear a noise*. New York: Dutton.
Repeated language patterns. A few difficult words (*against, ashamed, business*).

Gordon, J. R. 1991. *Six sleepy sheep*. Honesdale, PA: Caroline.
Alliterative, repetitive language.

Hale, S. J. 1984. *Mary had a little lamb*. New York: Holiday House.
Familiar rhyme; some difficult words (*against, eager, lingered*). Two to four lines/phrases per page; two pages have four short lines each.

Hawkins, C., and J. Hawkins. 1986. *Max and the magic word*. New York: Viking Kestrel.
Repetitive language pattern. One or two sentences per page; one page has three sentences.

Hayes, S. 1986. *This is the bear*. Philadelphia, PA: Lippincott.
Rhyming, repetitive language; cumulative story. Two lines per page; one page has eight lines.

Heller, N. 1994. *Ten old pails*. New York: Greenwillow.
Familiar sequence (counting); a few difficult words (*launch, syrup*). Most pages have two or fewer sentences on one to four lines.

Henley, C. 1991. *Farm day*. New York: Dial.
Companion book to Henley's *Stormy Day* (see the following list).

Johnson, A. 1991. *One of three*. Danbury, CT: Orchard.
Repetitive language; African-American characters. Some difficult words (*apartment, bakery, invited, remember*). One or two sentences on two to four lines per page.

Lawson, C. 1991. *Teddy bear, teddy bear*. New York: Dial.
Familiar nursery rhyme. One or two sentences on two to four lines per page. Invites movement/participation.

Lewis, R. 1987. *Hello Mr. Scarecrow*. New York: Farrar, Straus, and Giroux.
Familiar sequence (months of the year). A few difficult words (*harvested, plodded*).

Lewison, W. C. 1992. *Going to sleep on the farm*. New York: Dial.
Question-answer format; rhyming, repetitive language pattern.

Maris, R. 1982. *Better move on, frog!* London: Julia MacRae/Franklin Watts.
Repetitive language pattern.

Maris, R. 1986. *I wish I could fly*. New York: Greenwillow.
Repetitive language pattern; cumulative text. One or two lines per page; two pages have four short lines each.

Maris, R. 1988. *Hold tight, bear!* New York: Delacorte.
Close text-picture match.

McBratney, S. 1996. *The caterpillow fight*. Cambridge, MA: Candlewick.
Rhyming language.

Merriam, E. 1993. *12 ways to get to 11*. New York: Simon and Schuster.
Familiar sequence (counting); some difficult words. One or two sentences on one to nine short lines per page.

Miller, J. 1983. *Farm counting book*. New York: Prentice-Hall.
Familiar sequence (counting); the second half of the book is in a question-answer format.

Miller, V. 1993. *Go to bed!* Cambridge, MA: Candlewick.
Repetitive language pattern. Most pages have one or two sentences on one or two lines; one page has three sentences.

Morris, A. 1989. *Bread, bread, bread*. New York: Mulberry.
Features breads from many countries.

Nikola-Lisa, W. 1991. *1, 2, 3, Thanksgiving!* Warsaw, IN: Whitman.
Familiar sequence (counting); close text-picture match. Some difficult words (*balances, measures, sparkling, squishes*).

Peek, M. 1985. *Mary wore her red dress and Henry wore his green sneakers*. New York: Clarion/Ticknor & Fields.
Repetitive language patterns; text based on old folk song; close text-picture match.

Polushkin, M. 1988. *Kitten in trouble*. New York: Bradbury.
Includes a refrain. One or two sentences on one to four lines per page.

Polushkin, M. 1990. *Here's that kitten*. New York: Bradbury.
Repeated language.

Pomerantz, C. 1989. *Flap your wings and try*. New York: Greenwillow.
Rhyming text; repeated phrases. Two sentences or fewer per page; one page has three sentences.

Raffi. 1987. *Shake my sillies out.* New York: Crown.
Predictable, repetitive, rhythmic language pattern. Invites movement/participation.

Rockwell, A. 1984. *Trucks.* New York: Dutton.

Rockwell, A. 1989. *Apples and pumpkins.* New York: Macmillan.
One or two sentences on one to five lines per page.

Rockwell, A. 1989. *Bear child's book of special days.* New York: Dutton.
Familiar holidays and sequence (months of the year). One or two sentences on one to five lines per page.

Root, P. 1996. *One windy Wednesday.* Cambridge, MA: Candlewick Press.
Repetitive language with good picture cues. One or two sentences per page; one page has three sentences.

Samton, S. W. 1987. *Beside the bay.* New York: Philomel.
Rhyming text with close text-picture match.

Samton, S. W. 1993. *Oh, no! A naptime adventure.* New York: Viking.
Rhyming text with repeated phrase throughout.

Scott, A. H. 1992. *On mother's lap.* New York: Clarion.
Repetitive language pattern. Inuit (Eskimo) characters. One or two sentences on one to six lines per page.

Shaw, N. 1986. *Sheep in a Jeep*.* Boston: Houghton Mifflin.
Predictable language pattern; rhyming text. Close text-picture match.

(*Jeep® is a registered trademark of Daimler Chrysler Corporation.)

Shaw, N. 1991. *Sheep in a shop.* Boston: Houghton Mifflin.
Predictable language pattern; rhyming text. Close text-picture match.

Shaw, N. 1992. *Sheep out to eat.* Boston: Houghton Mifflin.
Predictable language pattern; rhyming text. Close text-picture match; some difficult words (*appetites, custard, spinach, waiters*).

Sis, P. 1993. *Komodo!* New York: Greenwillow.
Features information on Komodo dragons; some difficult words.

Tolstoy, A. 1968. *The great big enormous turnip.* Danbury, CT: Watts.
Predictable, cumulative tale. One or two sentences on one to seven lines per page; one page has three sentences.

Van Laan, N. 1990. *A mouse in my house.* New York: Knopf.
Repetitive, rhyming language pattern. Two sentences on four lines or fewer per page.

Voake, C. 1989. *Mrs. Goose's baby.* New York: Little, Brown.
A few difficult words (*cuddled, different, shore, strangers*). Most pages have one or two sentences; one page has five sentences.

Walsh, E. S. 1989. *Mouse paint.* San Diego, CA: Harcourt Brace Jovanovich.
A concept book about colors.

Walsh, E. S. 1991. *Mouse count.* San Diego, CA: Harcourt Brace Jovanovich.
Familiar sequence (counting); repeated language patterns.

Walsh, E. S. 1993. *Hop jump.* San Diego, CA: Harcourt Brace Jovanovich.
Repeated language patterns.

Weiss, N. 1989. *Where does the brown bear go?* New York: Greenwillow.
Rhythmic, repetitive language patterns. One or two sentences on one to four lines per page.

Weiss, N. 1990. *An egg is an egg.* New York: G. P. Putnam's Sons.
Repetitive language patterns; rhyming text.

Weiss, N. 1992. *On a hot, hot day.* New York: G. P. Putnam's Sons.
Repetitive, rhyming language patterns. Story set in a Latino neighborhood. Two or fewer sentences on one to three lines per page.

Wellington, M. 1992. *Mr. cookie baker.* New York: Dutton.

Wells, R. 1973. *Noisy Nora.* New York: Dial.
Rhyming text; repetitive phrases.

West, C. 1987. *Hello, great big bullfrog!* New York: Harper and Row.
Repetitive language pattern; cumulative tale. One or two sentences per page; one page has three sentences.

Westcott, N. B. 1987. *Peanut butter and jelly: A play rhyme.* New York: Dutton.
Familiar song; repetitive language pattern. Invites participation.

Westcott, N. B. 1989. *Skip to my Lou.* Boston: Joy Street/Little, Brown.
Familiar rhyme.

Wood, D., and A. Wood. 1984. *The little mouse, the red ripe strawberry, and the big hungry bear.* New York: Child's Play.
Repeated phrases throughout; a few difficult words (*disguised, especially, guarding*).

Wood, J. 1991. *Dads are such fun.* New York: Simon and Schuster.
Repeated phrase throughout. Most pages have one or two sentences; one page has four sentences.

Wood, J. 1992. *Moo moo, brown cow.* San Diego, CA: Harcourt Brace Jovanovich.
Repetitive language pattern; familiar sequence (counting).

Zolotow, C. 1958. *Do you know what I'll do?* New York: Harper and Row.
Repetitive language pattern.

Zolotow, C. 1958. *Sleepy book.* New York: Harper and Row.
Some difficult words.

Picture Books With Three or More Sentences per Page

Alborough, J. 1992. *Where's my teddy?* Cambridge, MA: Candlewick.
Predictable, rhyming text. One to four sentences per page.

Anholt, C., and L. Anholt. 1992. *All about you.* New York: Viking.
Question-answer format; close text-picture match; identification book.

Anholt, C., and L. Anholt. 1992. *Two by two.* Cambridge, MA: Candlewick.
Predictable due to close text-picture match; repeated words. One to three sentences on two to six short lines per page.

Aylesworth, J. 1992. *Old black fly.* New York: Holt.
Repetitive, rhythmic language pattern; familiar sequence (ABC). One to four short sentences per page.

Ballard, R. 1994. *Good-bye, house*. New York: Greenwillow.
Repeated phrase throughout. One to five sentences per page.

Bang, M. 1999. *When Sophie gets angry-really, really angry. . . .* New York: Blue Sky Press.
Vivid picture cues.

Barton, B. 1991. *The three bears*. New York: HarperCollins.
Familiar folktale. One to seven sentences/phrases per page.

Barton, B. 1993. *The little red hen*. New York: HarperCollins.
Familiar folktale. Predictable, repetitive language patterns.

Bennett, J. 1985. *Teeny tiny*. New York: Putnam.
Repetitive language pattern. One to seven short lines per page.

Blackburn, C. 1986. *Waiting for Sunday*. New York: Scholastic.
Familiar sequences (days of the week and counting). Predictable, rhyming, repetitive language patterns.

Bonsall, C. 1980. *Who's afraid of the dark?* New York: Harper and Row.
An early "I Can Read" book. Simple, illustrated text with multicultural pictures. One to four sentences on one to four lines per page.

Brown, R. 1985. *The big sneeze*. New York: Lothrop, Lee, and Shepard.
Repetitive language pattern; some difficult words (*shrieked, disturbed, captured, panicked*).

Brown, R. 1996. *Toad*. New York: Dutton.
Many fun, difficult words. One to four lines per page.

Bucknell, C. 1987. *One bear in the picture*. New York: Dial.
Rhythmic, rhyming, predictable story. Up to three sentences on up to four lines per page.

Burleigh, R. 1999. *It's funny where Ben's train takes him*. Danbury, CT: Orchard.
Rhyming language and a refrain.

Burningham, J. 1971. *Mr. Gumpy's outing*. New York: Holt.
Predictable plot.

Caines, J. 1973. *Abby*. New York: Harper and Row.
Limited text story about adoption. African-American characters and author. One to five lines per page.

Caines, J. 1988. *I need a lunch box*. New York: HarperCollins.
Familiar sequence (days of the week); some difficult words (*collection, counter, sandwiches, sneakers*). African-American characters, author, and illustrator.

Calmenson, S. 1991. *Dinner at the panda palace*. New York: HarperCollins.
Predictable, rhyming text; familiar sequence (counting); close text-picture match. Some difficult words (*elegant, enormously, graciously, hyena*).

Calmenson, S. 1992. *Zip, whiz, zoom!* New York: Little, Brown.
Rhythmic, rhyming text.

Carle, E. 1981. *The very hungry caterpillar*. New York: Putnam.
Familiar sequence (number story).

Carlstrom, N. W. 1990. *Moose in the garden.* New York: Harper and Row.
Rhythmic text with repeated phrases throughout; some difficult words (*broccoli, cauliflower, cabbage*). One to three sentences per page; last page has eight sentences.

Carlstrom, N. W. 1992. *Baby-o.* New York: Little, Brown.
Cumulative, repetitive, rhyming tale; language play. West Indian characters. Up to five short lines per page.

Carter, D. 1992. *Over in the meadow: An old counting rhyme.* New York: Scholastic.
Familiar rhyme and sequence (counting); some difficult words. Four sentences on four lines per page.

Carter, M., and C. Wright. 1989. *Go away, William!* New York: Macmillan.
Includes a refrain. One to three sentences on one to six short lines per page.

Causley, C. 1970. *"Quack!" said the billy-goat.* New York: Harper and Row.
Rhyming text. One to three sentences on one to five lines per page.

Child, L. M. 1993. *Over the river and through the woods.* New York: Harper Collins.
Familiar Thanksgiving rhyme; a few difficult words (*extremely, sleigh*). One to three sentences on one to five lines per page.

Christelow, E. 1992. *Five little monkeys sitting in a tree.* New York: Clarion.
Repetitive text; familiar sequence (counting). One to four sentences per page.

Cole, J. 1989. *It's too noisy!* New York: Crowell.
Repetitive language patterns. Retelling of a Jewish folktale. Up to seven sentences per page.

Cooper, H. 1993. *The bear under the stairs.* New York: Dial.
Repetitive, rhyming language patterns. Some difficult words. One to eight lines per page.

Crebbin, J. 1996. *Into the castle.* Cambridge, MA: Candlewick.
Repetitive, rhyming language patterns. Some difficult words. Up to four lines per page.

Degen, B. 1983. *Jamberry.* New York: HarperCollins.
Rhythmic, rhyming text with the word *berry* repeated throughout. One to six short lines per page.

Degen, B. 1991. *Teddy bear towers.* New York: HarperCollins.
Rhythmic, rhyming text. One to eight lines on one to five short sentences per page.

Edwards, P. D. 1996. *Some smug slug.* New York: HarperCollins.
Fun, alliterative language; many difficult words. One to four lines per page.

Ehlert, L. 1991. *Red leaf, yellow leaf.* San Diego, CA: Harcourt Brace Jovanovich.
Some difficult words. Contains detailed information about tree parts and tree planting at the end. Three sentences or fewer per page.

Ehlert, L. 1993. *Nuts to you!* San Diego, CA: Harcourt Brace Jovanovich.
Rhyming text; close text-picture match. A few difficult words (*awhile, rather, steal, wait*).

English, T. 1993. *Old MacDonald had a farm: A lift and look counting book*. Racine, WI: Western.
Familiar song/rhyme and familiar sequence (counting); repetitive language pattern. One to seven short lines per page.

Ericsson, J. A. 1993. *No milk*. New York: Tambourine/Morrow.
Includes a refrain. One to four short sentences on one to five lines per page.

Flack, M. 1932. *Ask Mr. Bear*. New York: Macmillan.
Predictable, cumulative story.

Fox, M. 1986. *Hattie and the fox*. New York: Bradbury.
Cumulative tale; repetitive language pattern.

Fox, M. 1988. *Guess what?* New York: Gulliver.
Predictable question-answer format.

Galdone, P. 1986. *Over in the meadow*. New York: Prentice-Hall.
Familiar rhyme; familiar sequence.

Garten, J. 1994. *The alphabet tale*. New York: Greenwillow.
ABC book. Rhyming text with question-answer format; excellent for predicting story events at page turns. Has many difficult words.

Gay, M. L. 1999. *Stella, star of the sea*. Toronto, Canada: Groundwood Books.

Giganti, P., Jr. 1988. *How many snails? A counting book*. New York: Greenwillow.
Familiar sequence (counting); predictable, repetitive language patterns. Close text-picture match with counting questions. One phrase and three questions per page; last page has two sentences.

Ginsburg, M. 1980. *Good morning chick*. New York: Greenwillow.
Repetitive language pattern.

Gliori, D. 1991. *New big sister*. New York: Bradbury Press.
Some difficult words.

Gliori, D. 1992. *My little brother*. Cambridge, MA: Candlewick Press.
Some difficult words. Six sentences or fewer per page.

Greenfield, E. 1977. *Africa dream*. New York: HarperCollins.
Depicts African culture; some difficult words. African-American author and illustrator. Most pages have two to four lines; the last page has eight short lines.

Grejniec, M. 1993. *Look*. New York: North-South.
Repeated word throughout; some difficult words. Polish author. One to four sentences on one to five lines per page.

Grossman, V. 1991. *Ten little rabbits*. San Francisco, CA: Chronicle.
Counting book; rhythmic, rhyming language. Features Native American culture. One line per page; has many advanced words.

Guarino, D. 1989. *Is your mama a llama?* New York: Scholastic.
Repetitive, rhyming story pattern. Good for predicting story events at page turns.

Hawkins, C., and J. Hawkins. 1987. *I know an old lady who swallowed a fly*. New York: Putnam.
Familiar, cumulative rhyme.

Hayes, S. 1988. *This is the bear and the picnic lunch.* Boston: Joy Street/Little, Brown.
Rhythmic, rhyming, cumulative text. One to four lines per page; one page has eight short lines.

Hayes, S. 1990. *Nine ducks nine.* New York: Lothrop, Lee, and Shepard.
Familiar sequence (counting); repetitive language pattern. One to three sentences on one to four lines per page.

Hayes, S. 1992. *This is the bear and the scary night.* Boston: Joy Street/Little, Brown.
Rhythmic, rhyming, cumulative text. One to four lines per page; one page has eight short lines.

Hellen, N. 1990. *Old MacDonald had a farm.* Danbury, CT: Orchard.
Familiar rhyme; repetitive language pattern.

Henley, C. 1993. *Stormy day.* Winnipeg, Canada: Hyperion.
Companion book to Henley's Farm Day (see the preceding list). Two to three sentences on two to six lines per page.

Hennessy, B. G. 1992. *Sleep tight.* New York: Viking.
Rhyming text with repetitive language. One to four lines per page.

Hutchins, P. 1972. *Good-night, owl.* New York: Macmillan.
Predictable plot; repetitive, cumulative story. Some difficult words (*chittered, cooed, screamed, starlings*). One or two sentences per page, but one page has eight sentences on sixteen lines.

Hutchins, P. 1976. *Don't forget the bacon!* New York: Greenwillow.
Repetitive language pattern. One to five lines per page.

Hutchins, P. 1991. *The surprise party.* New York: Aladdin.
Repetitive language patterns; several difficult words (*flea, hoeing, parsley, poultry, raiding, suppose*). One to four sentences on one to four lines per page.

Hutchins, P. 1992. *Silly Billy.* New York: Greenwillow.
Predictable, repetitive language pattern. One to four sentences per page.

Inkpen, M. 1991. *Kipper.* New York: Little, Brown.
Some difficult words. One to seven sentences per page.

Inkpen, M. 1992. *Kipper's toybox.* New York: Gulliver/Harcourt Brace Jovanovich.
Some difficult words. One to eight sentences per page.

Jeram, A. 1991. *It was Jake!* New York: Little, Brown.
Easy vocabulary; predictable plot with repeated language pattern.

Jeram, A. 1995. *Contrary Mary.* Cambridge, MA: Candlewick.
Good picture cues. One to five sentences per page.

Jones, C. 1989. *Old MacDonald had a farm.* Boston: Houghton Mifflin.
Familiar song/rhyme; repetitive language pattern. Close text-picture match. Good for predicting story events at page turns. One to six lines per page.

Jones, C. 1990. *This old man.* Boston: Houghton Mifflin.
Familiar counting rhyme; repetitive language pattern. Three to four lines per page.

Kalan, R. 1981. *Jump, frog, jump!* New York: Greenwillow.
Cumulative tale; repetitive language pattern; question-answer format.

Keats, E. J. 1967. *Peter's chair*. New York: Harper and Row.
Illustrations are of African-Americans. Some difficult words (*arranged, fussing, muttered, quietly*). One to four sentences per page.

Kraus, R. 1987. *Come out and play, little mouse*. New York: Greenwillow.
Repetitive language pattern; familiar sequence (days of the week). One to four short lines (up to three sentences) per page.

Kudrna, C. I. 1986. *To bathe a boa*. Minneapolis, MN: Carolrhoda.
Rhythmic, rhyming text. Several difficult words. One to three sentences on one to four lines per page.

Langstaff, J. 1974. *Oh, a-hunting we will go*. New York: Atheneum.
Repetitive, rhyming, predictable text; close text-picture match. Some difficult words (*armadillo, chorus*). Two to four lines per page.

Lillegard, D. 1989. *Sitting in my box*. New York: Dutton.
Repetitive story pattern; close text-picture match. Jungle animal names supported by pictures. One to four short sentences per page.

Lillie, P. 1989. *Jake and Rosie*. New York: Greenwillow.
Interracial friendship portrayed. One to four sentences on one to five lines per page.

Lindbergh, R. 1993. *There's a COW in the road!* New York: Dial.
Repetitive, rhyming text; some difficult words.

Little, J., and M. deVries. 1991. *Once upon a golden apple*. New York: Viking.
Repetitive language patterns; familiar fairy tale and nursery rhyme images. Some difficult words. One to six lines per page. Invites participation.

Lloyd, D. 1986. *The sneeze*. Philadelphia, PA: Lippincott.
Question-answer format; repeated language throughout. One to eight sentences per page.

Lobel, Arnold. 1981. *On market street*. New York: Greenwillow.
ABC book. Close text-picture match; some difficult words. Beginning and end of book have seven to nine lines on a page; the rest of the text has one word per page.

Macdonald, M. 1991. *Rosie's baby tooth*. New York: Atheneum.
One to eight short sentences per page.

Macdonald, M. 1990. *Rosie runs away*. New York: Atheneum.
One to seven short sentences on one to ten lines per page.

Martin, B., Jr. 1993. *Old devil wind*. San Diego, CA: Harcourt Brace Jovanovich.
Repetitive, cumulative language pattern. One to five sentences per page. Invites participation.

Martin, B., Jr., and J. Archambault. 1989. *Chicka chicka boom boom*. New York: Simon and Schuster.
ABC book. Rhythmic, rhyming, predictable text.

Morgenstern, C. 1991. *Good night, feet.* New York: Holt.
Rhyming text with repeated phrase throughout. One to five sentences on one to six lines per page.

Noble, T. H. 1980. *The day Jimmy's boa ate the wash.* New York: Dial.
Close text-picture match. One to six sentences per page.

Nodset, J. L. 1963. *Who took the farmer's hat?* New York: Harper and Row.
Repetitive language. One to five sentences on one to five lines per page.

Omerod, J. 1993. *Midnight pillow fight.* Cambridge, MA: Candlewick.
Repeated language patterns. One to four lines per page.

Paul, K., and P. Carter. 1989. *Captain Teachum's buried treasure.* New York: Oxford.
Repeated language pattern.

Pearson, T. C. 1991. *The howling dog.* New York: Farrar, Straus, and Giroux.
Repetitive language; a few difficult words.

Pizer, A. 1990. *It's a perfect day.* Philadelphia, PA: Lippincott.
Repetitive language patterns; cumulative tale. Contains rebus sentences. One to ten short sentences per page.

Polushkin, M. 1984. *Mama's secret.* Salem, OR: Four Winds.
Repeated language. One to four sentences per page.

Polushkin, M. 1988. *Who said meow?* New York: Bradbury.
Repeated language. One to four short sentences per page.

Pomerantz, C. 1984. *One duck, another duck.* New York: Greenwillow.
Familiar sequence (counting). One to six short sentences per page.

Prater, J. 1991. *No! Said Joe.* Cambridge, MA: Candlewick.
Predictable, rhyming, repetitive language patterns. Some difficult words (*disgusting, dreadful, naughty*). Most pages have five lines.

Raschka, C. 1992. *Charlie Parker played be bop.* Danbury, CT: Jackson/Orchard/Watts.
Brief, rhythmic/musical text; language play. Some difficult words (*barbeque, music, saxophone*). Features an African-American character.

Reiser, L. 1992. *Any kind of dog.* New York: Greenwillow.
Simple text with predictable, repetitive language patterns. One to four phrases/sentences on one to six lines per page.

Rice, E. 1977. *Sam who never forgets.* New York: Greenwillow.
Predictable plot.

Rice, E. 1981. *Benny bakes a cake.* New York: Greenwillow.
Predictable plot. One to four short sentences per page.

Rockwell, A. 1988. *Hugo at the window.* New York: Macmillan.
Repeated language patterns. One to five sentences per page.

Rosen, M. 1989. *We're going on a bear hunt.* New York: McElderry.
Predictable, repetitive language pattern. Three to six lines per page. Invites participation, movement, and drama.

Rounds, G. 1990. *I know an old lady who swallowed a fly*. New York: Holiday House.
Predictable, repetitive language patterns. Rhyming, cumulative text. Two to six sentences per page.

Sage, J. 1990. *To sleep*. New York: McElderry.
Repeated language; some difficult words (*beyond, darling, reached*). One to four sentences per page.

Saunders, D., and J. Saunders. 1990. *Dibble and dabble*. New York: Bradbury.
Predictable, repetitive language pattern; some difficult words.

Serfozo, M. 1989. *Who wants one?* New York: McElderry.
Familiar sequence (counting); rhyming text with repetitive language. One to five sentences per page.

Shaw, N. 1989. *Sheep on a ship*. Boston: Houghton Mifflin.
Predictable language pattern; rhyming text.

Smalls-Hector, I. 1992. *Jonathan and his mommy*. New York: Little, Brown.
Some rhyming phrases; close text-picture match. African-American characters and author. Invites movement and drama.

Tolhurst, M. 1990. *Somebody and the three blairs*. Danbury, CT: Orchard.
A new twist on the familiar Goldilocks story. Some difficult words (*escaped, naughty*). One to five sentences per page.

Tompert, A. 1993. *Just a little bit*. Boston: Houghton Mifflin.
Repeated language throughout; several difficult words. One to six sentences per page.

Trapani, I. 1993. *The itsy bitsy spider*. Watertown, MA: Whispering Coyote.
Familiar rhyme; repeated language patterns. One to three short sentences on two to four lines per page.

Udry, J. M. 1981. *Thump and plunk*. New York: HarperCollins.
Repetitive language. One to seven sentences on one to nine lines per page.

Van Laan, N. 1987. *The big fat worm*. New York: Knopf.
Predictable, repetitive story pattern. One to six lines per page.

Voake, C. 1986. *Tom's cat*. New York: Harper and Row.
Question-answer pattern with repetitive language. A few difficult words (*cleaning, knitting, quickly*). Four or fewer sentences per page.

Waddell, M. 1991. *Squeak-a-lot*. New York: Greenwillow.
Repeated phrases throughout. One to five sentences per page.

Waddell, M. 1992. *Owl babies*. Cambridge, MA: Candlewick.
Repetitive language pattern. One to eight lines per page.

Waddell, M. 1992. *Sailor bear*. Cambridge, MA: Candlewick.
Repeated phrases throughout. One to five sentences per page.

Wahl, J. 1992. *My cat Ginger*. New York: Tambourine.
Some repetitive language; some difficult words. One to eight short sentences per page.

Walsh, E. S. 1992. *You silly goose*. San Diego, CA: Harcourt Brace Jovanovich.

Weeks, S. 1998. *Mrs. McNosh hangs up her wash*. New York: HarperFestival. Rhyming text.

Williams, L. 1986. *The little old lady who was not afraid of anything*. New York: Harper.
Cumulative tale. Invites participation, movement, and drama.

Wilson, E. 1993. *Music in the night*. New York: Cobblehill.
Repetitive language pattern; cumulative story. One to four sentences on one to eight lines per page.

Wolff, A. 1985. *Only the cat saw*. New York: Dodd.
Repetitive language. Two to four sentences on four to six lines per page.

Wood, A. 1984. *The napping house*. San Diego, CA: Harcourt Brace Jovanovich.
Cumulative tale; repetitive language pattern. Some difficult words.

Wood, A. 1985. *King Bidgood's in the bathtub*. San Diego, CA: Harcourt Brace Jovanovich.
Predictable, repetitive language patterns. One to four lines per page.

Yolen, J. 1993. *Mouse's birthday*. New York: G. P. Putnam's Sons.
Repetitive, rhyming language pattern. One to four short sentences per page.

Young, E. 1992. *Seven blind mice*. New York: Philomel.
Familiar sequence (counting and days of the week); cumulative story; some difficult words.

Ziefert, H. 1990. *Who can boo the loudest?* New York: Harper and Row.
Predictable, repetitive language patterns. One to five sentences per page.

Zimmerman, A. 1999. *Trashy town*. New York: HarperCollins.
Repetitive, rhyming language that invites participation. One to four short sentences per page.

CHAPTER FOUR:
Teaching Daily Lessons

Teacher-Directed PALS lessons are presented to students by following specific formats for each activity. These formats are presented on the Daily Teaching Format Guide forms at the end of this Chapter. The Daily Teaching Format Guides provide scripts you can use for teaching each lesson. There are three Daily Teaching Format Guides: one for Lessons 1-15, one for Lessons 16-36, and one for Lessons 37-57. Use the appropriate Guide to present each lesson, simply inserting items from that day's Lesson Sheet and storybook as indicated. Thus, to teach a lesson all you need is (1) the Lesson Sheet for that day, (2) the Story Sharing storybook for that day, and (3) the appropriate Daily Teaching Format Guide. Although the Lesson Sheets and storybooks change each day, each Daily Teaching Format Guide is used again and again.

Each day, the basic format remains the same, even though the content of each lesson changes. All three formats are designed to reduce the amount of teacher talk and increase the amount of student talk during each lesson. Likewise, the use of phrases that the students hear every day reduces the chance that they will become confused by unclear language. The structure provided by daily repeating formats is comforting to students who often may be confused by the constantly changing environment found in most classrooms. The words scripted in the Daily Teaching Format Guides have been shown to communicate clearly to students, thereby reducing the guesswork of figuring out how to explain concepts to struggling learners.

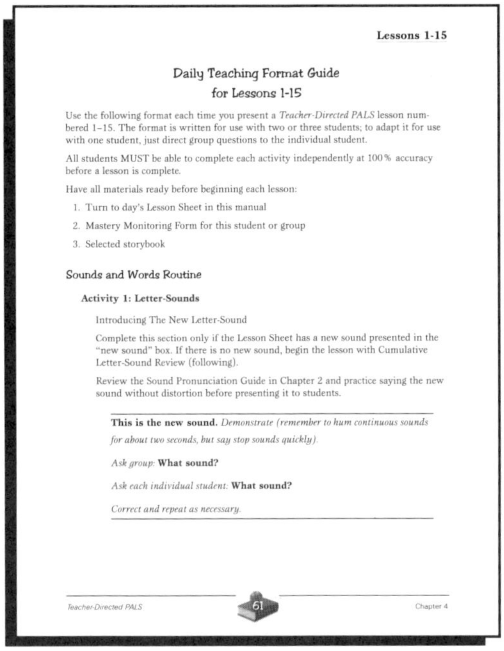

The Formats

Each format is much like a script of a play, in that the teaching behaviors and the words that you say to students for each activity are specified in the Format Guide (see Figure 6). For each activity, a teaching script is provided and is placed inside a box. Text written outside the boxes is instructional material or reminders pertaining to the activity, but text inside the box is what you actually say to or do with your students. Text written in boldface indicates the actual words you say to students; text in italics provides you with directions for presenting information from the Lesson Sheet or storybook.

FIGURE 6A
DAILY TEACHING FORMAT GUIDE

FIGURE 6B
DAILY TEACHING FORMAT GUIDE

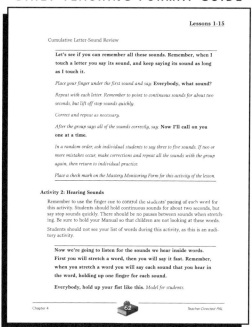

with corresponds to the lesson number that you are teaching.

Formats for the Sounds and Words Routine

Letter-Sounds Activity

The teaching format for this activity consists of two parts: Introducing the New Letter-Sound and Cumulative Letter-Sound Review.

Introducing the New Letter-Sound (Lessons 1-57)

In lessons in which a new letter-sound correspondence is presented to your students for the first time, you will need to directly teach the sound represented by the letter. The new sound will be located in a box on the Lesson Sheet. The letter for that sound is printed inside the box (see Figure 7).

FIGURE 7
LETTER-SOUNDS ACTIVITY WITH A NEW SOUND

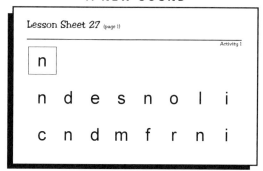

Each day on which a boxed letter appears on the Lesson Sheet, you should first model for the students how to pronounce the new sound. Have the students then say the sound with you, then have them say it by themselves in unison. Last, have each individual student tell you the sound that

There are three teaching formats in *Teacher-Directed PALS*, which correspond to three clusters of lessons: Lessons 1-15, Lessons 16-36, and Lessons 37-57. The Daily Lesson Format Guide changes to correspond with changes in the lessons. For example, at Lesson 16 students are asked to sight read words that they have previously sounded out. They also read the passage from sight rather than sounding out every word. Beginning at Lesson 37, the Hearing Sounds activity disappears from the lesson sequence and the Letter-Sounds activity is only practiced once. Also beginning at Lesson 37, students sound out words by syllable rather than by letter. Commensurate with these changes, the Passage Reading activity becomes lengthier. Because what you say and do during each lesson is written for you on the Daily Teaching Format Guide, you do not need to memorize which lessons these changes will happen in. You simply need to make sure that the Format Guide you are teaching the new letter represents. If there is no new sound for the day, then you should begin the day's lesson with the Cumulative Letter-Sound Review (following).

The basic format for presenting the new letter's sound is as follows:

This is the new sound. *Demonstrate (remember to hum continuous sounds for about two seconds, but say stop sounds quickly).*

Ask group. **What sound?**

Ask each individual student: **What sound?**

Correct and repeat as necessary.

Cumulative Letter-Sound Review (Lessons 1-57)

During Cumulative Letter-Sound Review, students will practice automatic recognition of the sounds represented by letters. To practice recognizing letter-sound correspondences, you will hold up the day's Lesson Sheet with the letter-sound review in front of the students so that they can all see the page (see Figure 8). Next, touch each letter-sound correspondence written on the Lesson Sheet and ask *all* students in the group to tell you that letter's sound in unison. Students should be told to say the sound for as long as you touch it. You should keep your finger underneath continuous sounds for about two seconds, but lift quickly from stop sounds. After you have reviewed all of the letters in the Letter-Sounds section of the Lesson Sheet,

you should then ask individual students to tell you the letter-sound correspondences of several letters.

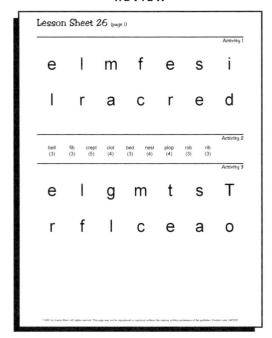

FIGURE 8
CUMULATIVE LETTER-SOUND REVIEW

The basic format for presenting the Cumulative Letter-Sound Review is as follows:

Let's see if you can remember all these sounds. Remember, when I touch a letter you say its sound, and keep saying its sound as long as I touch it.

Place your finger under the first sound and say: **Everybody, what sound?**

Repeat with each letter. Remember to point to continuous sounds for about two seconds, but lift off stop sounds quickly.

Correct and repeat as necessary.

After the group says all of the sounds correctly, say: **Now I'll call on you one at a time.**

In a random order, ask individual students to say three to five sounds. If two or more mistakes occur, make corrections and repeat all the sounds with the group again, then return to individual practice.

Place a check mark on the Mastery Monitoring Form for this activity of the lesson.

Hearing Sounds Activity (Lessons 1-36)

If students are to blend letter-sounds that they see visually to sound out words, they must first be able to segment (stretch) and put back together (blend) words they hear. During Hearing Sounds, you will say a word at the normal rate and ask students to "stretch the word." In this activity, students will hold up one finger for each phoneme or sound in the word. You should also hold up a finger for each sound in order to control the pace of instruction; however, you should *not* say the sounds out loud (let the students do it by themselves). After the students have stretched the word, isolating each phoneme, you should then ask them to say the word at a normal rate.

Use the following *finger cue* when words are stretched. It is a visual aid to help make more concrete for students the very abstract concept that words have individual sounds within them. Basically it consists of holding up one finger for each sound. The specific steps are:

1. Hold your right fist up with the back of your hand facing the class. Your hand should be about as high as your shoulder (or a little higher if that is more comfortable). Ask all the students in the group to raise their fists just like yours.

2. Raise your index finger as soon as the students say the first sound in the word. Do *not* say the sound yourself. Keep that finger raised throughout the entire word.

3. Raise your middle finger as soon as the students say the second sound heard in the word. Again, do *not* say the sound yourself. Keep your index and middle fingers raised throughout the rest of the word.

4. Repeat the process for any remaining sounds. The majority of words used in this book's lessons will have two to four phonemes.

When using this finger cue, it is important that you hold your hand up so all the students can see it clearly. Also, be sure to raise your fingers at the exact time you want the students to say the next phoneme, and be sure to hold your fingers up distinctly; that is, there should be no question in the students' minds if a finger is up or down.

The basic format for presenting the Hearing Sounds activity is as follows:

Now we're going to listen for the sounds we hear inside words. First you will stretch a word, then you will say it fast. Remember, when you stretch a word you will say each sound that you hear in the word, holding up one finger for each sound.

Everybody, hold up your fist like this. *Model for students.*

First word. *(Insert from Lesson Sheet.)* **Stretch.** *(Insert from Lesson Sheet.)*

Hold up one finger for each sound, but do NOT say the sound yourself. Students should not say the next sound until you hold up the next finger.

What word did you stretch? *(Wait for students to answer.)* **Yes,** *(insert from Lesson Sheet).*

Next word.

Repeat the process with each word listed on the Lesson Sheet for Activity 2. Correct and repeat as necessary.

After the group stretches all the words correctly, say: **Now I'll call on you one at a time.**

Each student should segment and blend two to three words with 100 % accuracy.

Place a check mark on the Mastery Monitoring Form for this activity of the lesson.

Sounding Out Activity Lessons 1-57

Students practice sounding out words in all 57 lessons. However, starting at Lesson 16, students also practice reading words from sight after they have sounded the words out. At Lesson 36, students move from sounding out letter-by-letter to reading units or chunks within words. Although most students find this skill fairly easy, some find learning to sound out words more difficult. To make sounding out easier for students, *PALS* builds directly upon the Hearing Sounds activity (i.e., Segmenting and Blending). The big difference is that in Sounding Out, students have to produce the sound for the letter they see, rather than identifying the sound they hear as in Hearing Sounds. The teaching format for this activity consists of two parts: Sounding Out Words, Then Reading Them and Reading the Words Fast.

Sounding Out Words, Then Reading Them (Lessons 1-36)

In *Teacher-Directed PALS*, students are taught to sound out words by saying the sound for each letter as you touch a dot that is positioned under each letter-sound correspondence. Students are also taught to stretch each sound for as long as you point to the dot under the letter. Students are taught not to stop between sounds, but to stretch or hum the word.

The format for presenting Sounding Out Words, Then Reading Them is as follows:

Now you're going to sound out words, then you'll read them. When I touch the dot under a letter, you say its sound and keep saying its sound until I touch the dot under the next letter. You will not stop between sounds; you will hum the word.

Place your fingertip beside the first word.

Sound it out.

Slide your finger under each letter, pointing to each dot in turn. Point to continuous sounds for about two seconds, but move off of stop sounds quickly. There should be no pauses between sounds when sounding out.

Correct and repeat as necessary.

Read it.

Repeat for each word.

After the group sounds out all of the words correctly, say: **Now I'll call on you one at a time.**

In a random order, ask individual

---

students to sound out and then read one or two words.

If two or more mistakes occur, make corrections and repeat all the words with the group again, then return to individual practice.

Place a check mark on the Mastery Monitoring Form for this activity of the lesson.

Reading the Words Fast (Lessons 16-36)

Beginning with Lesson 16, students will not only sound out each word listed on the Lesson Sheet, but they will also read the entire list from sight. This is called Reading the Words Fast.

The format for Reading the Words Fast is:

Good sounding out. Now let's read these words fast.

Point to the first word.

When I tap next to a word, you tell me the word. I'll give you think time, so wait for me to tap.

First word. *(Think time should be one to three seconds, depending on students' ability.)*

What word? *(Tap. Wait for students to answer.)*

Point to the next word. **Next word.**

Repeat with entire list. In a random order, ask individuals to read several words fast. If an error occurs, return to sounding out and saying the word fast. Then return to individual practice. If more than two errors occur, repeat sounding out format with entire group before continuing to read the words fast.

_____

Chunking (Lesson 37-57)

Beginning at Lesson 37, students will no longer sound out words. Instead, they read the syllable units (i.e., chunks) within words, then read the whole word. The procedure of reading each syllable as a unit is known as "chunking." For this activity, the sound chunks are underlined. The student's job is to read each sound chunk, then read the whole word fast. Single-syllable words are just read "fast first."

The format for Chunking is:

_____

Now we're going to read words in chunks, then we'll read them fast. Small words have only one chunk, so you'll read them fast first. For big words, you'll read each underlined chunk, then you'll read the whole word fast. When I touch an underlined part you'll read it. After you read each underlined part, you'll read the whole word fast.

(Point to the first word.) **First word.** *(Point to the first underlined part, and allow students one to two seconds of think time, as necessary.)* **Read the part.** *(Repeat with each additional underlined part.)*

Now, read the word. *(Quickly move your finger from left to right under the word.)*

Next word.

Repeat procedure with remaining words. If an error occurs in reading a chunk, sound out the chunk and then return to reading each chunk fast.

_____

After reading each word using the chunking procedure, the students should then read the list of words a second time fast, in the same manner that they read the word lists in Lessons 16-36.

_____

Good chunking. Now let's read these words fast.

Point to the first word.

When I tap on a word, you tell me the word. I'll give you think time, so wait for me to tap.

First word. *(Allow think time of one half to two seconds, depending on students' ability.)* **What word?** *(Tap.)*

Point to the next word.

Next word. *(Tap.)*

Repeat with entire list. In a random order, ask individuals to read several words the fast way. If an error occurs, return to the process of first chunking and then saying the word fast. If necessary, sound out a chunk, then return to individual practice. If more than two errors occur, repeat chunking format with entire group before continuing to read the words fast.

Sight Word Reading Activity (Lessons 1-57)

The Sight Word Reading activity has two parts: New Word, and Cumulative Sight Word Review.

The New Word

Each day in which a boxed word appears on the Lesson Sheet, you will first teach students to identify this word by sight. First you will tell the students what the word is, then they will say it by themselves in unison. Last, each individual student will read the new word independently.

The format for presenting the New Word is as follows:

Point to the new sight word and say:

We have a new word to learn to read today.

This word is *(insert from Lesson Sheet)*. **What's this word?** *(Wait for students to answer.)*

Yes, *(insert from Lesson Sheet)*.

Ask each individual student: **What's this word?**

Correct and repeat as necessary.

Cumulative Sight Word Review

During Cumulative Sight Word Review, students practice sight reading of previously taught high frequency words. To practice reading sight words, hold up the Lesson Sheet in front of the students so that they can all see the page. Next, place a fingertip beside each word and ask all students in the group to read it in unison. After you have reviewed all of the sight words on the Lesson Sheet, ask individual students to read several words.

The format for presenting the Cumulative Sight Word Review is as follows:

Now let's read the other words. When I point to a word, you read it.

Point to each sight word and ask: **What's this word?**

Repeat for each word.

After the group reads all of the words correctly, say: **Now I'll call on you one at a time.**

In a random order, ask individual students to read several words.

If two or more mistakes occur, make corrections and repeat all the words with the group again, then return to individual practice.

Place a check mark on the Mastery Monitoring Form for this activity of the lesson.

Passage Reading

During Passage Reading, students read connected text comprised either of words they have the skill to sound out or of previously taught high frequency sight words. Passage Reading provides the means for students to integrate these skills and to develop oral reading fluency.

There are two formats for teaching Passage Reading: One for Lessons 1-15 and one for Lessons 16-57. In Lessons 1-15, students sound out each word, then read it. To teach this format, you hold up the passage so that the students in the group can see it. You then use the sounding out cue of sliding your finger under each letter of a word, then asking students to read the word at normal rate. Then you ask individual students to read several sentences.

The format for presenting Passage Reading during Lessons 1-15 is as follows:

Now we're ready to read the story. When I point to a word you'll sound it out together, then read it fast. If it's a sight word, you'll just read it fast.

Point to the first word of the first sentence.

Sound it out.

Slide your finger under each letter, pointing to continuous sounds for about two seconds but moving off of stop sounds quickly. There should be no pauses between sounds when sounding out.

Correct and repeat as necessary.

Read it. *(Or, if the word is a sight word, say:* **You know this word. Read it.***)*

Sound out and read the entire story in unison. Remind students to wait until you point to a word.

Now I'll call on you one at a time.

Ask individual students to sound out and read two or three sentences independently. Correct and repeat as necessary.

Place a check mark on the Mastery Monitoring Form for this activity of the lesson.

Beginning with Lesson 16, students are asked to read each sentence without sounding out the words first. From then on, sounding out in text is only used if an error occurs. You control the fluency rate for reading each sentence by placing your fingertip under each word to cue students to read the word. Your goal in this is to pace the students so that they read each word as fast as they can, but without going so fast that the students can't keep up. Initially this means allowing up to three seconds of think time per word. However, by Lesson 57 students should be reading one word every second, or faster. How fast you will be able to pace Passage Reading will depend on the ability of individual students.

The format for presenting Passage Reading during Lessons 16-57 is as follows:

Now we're ready to read the story. When I point to a word you'll read it together. If you miss a word, we'll sound it out, then read it fast. We'll then read the sentence again.

First word.

Point to the first word. Allow think time of one to three seconds, depending on students' ability. Then lift your finger and move it to the next word. Wait the appropriate think time and move to the next word.

Read entire story in unison fashion, pointing to each word. If students do not read together, remind them to wait until you point to a word. After reading the

entire story together, ask individual students to read sentences independently.

Formats for the Story Sharing Routine

After completing the day's Sounds and Words routine, you should transition to Story Sharing. Story Sharing is conducted for the amount of time remaining in the session. Thus, you must determine how much time is left and gauge the pace of each activity accordingly. Also, the book chosen for Story Sharing should be short, in order to allow for varying amounts of time. To conduct Story Sharing, first hold up the book that you have selected for the day so that the students in the group can see the pictures and text. Then follow the formats in this section for teaching each activity (formats are the same for Lessons 1-57).

Pretend-Read

To conduct Pretend-Reading, focus the students' attention on the pictures on several pages of the storybook and ask students to make a few predictions about what they will read in the story. If students have difficulty making reasonable predictions, prompt them by focusing their attention on specific aspects of the pictures. Require students to state their predictions as complete sentences.

The format for Pretend-Reading is as follows:

Hold up the storybook so that all students in the group can see the cover.

Here's today's story. The title of this book is _____. *(Point to each word of the title as you read it.)* **It was written by _____. Now let's Pretend-Read this book. Remember that when we Pretend-Read a book, we look at the pictures and predict what we think the book is about.**

Turn to the starting page. Turn the book so that the students can see the pictures, and say: **Look at the pictures. What do you think is happening on these pages?** *Call on one student to answer.*

Quickly repeat this process on each page. Remember, Pretend-Reading should require no more than one to two minutes. Prompt students to attend to specific information in the pictures as necessary.

If students do not state a prediction as a complete sentence, model how to "say the whole sentence," and ask students to repeat the whole sentence.

Read Aloud

After quickly making predictions, you should read and reread the story quickly with the students. In the first reading, use echo reading: You read a sentence, then the students read the same sentence. On the second reading you should chorally read the story along with the students, allowing them to slightly lead the reading if possible and keeping your voice softer than on the first reading. On the third and final reading, ask the students to read the story independently, a sentence at a time. The format for presenting Read Aloud is as follows:

Step 1—Echo Read:

Now let's read this book. As we read it, check to see if any of your predictions about what happens in the story were right. We'll read this story several times. The first time I'll read a sentence, then you'll read the same sentence. Listen carefully and look at each word as I read it.

Turn back to the starting page and turn the book so that the students can see the text. Read the first sentence, pointing to each word as you read it, then say:

Your turn.

Guide students by pointing to each word as they read. If an error occurs, tell them the word and repeat the sentence.

Repeat this process through entire book.

Did any of your predictions come true? *Point out one or two that came true.*

<u>*Step 2—Choral Reading:*</u>

Now let's read the book again. This time we'll read the book together.

Read each sentence of the book in unison with the students. Read fairly slowly, and keep your voice low so that the students are leading. If students are trailing behind, slow down your reading rate.

<u>*Step 3—Independent Reading:*</u>

Now I'll call on you one at a time to read some of this story.

Ask each student to read a few sentences from the book aloud. If an error occurs, tell the student the word and ask him or her to reread the sentence. If the same student makes another error, tell the student the word and reread the sentence yourself, then ask the student to reread the sentence.

Excellent reading, everyone. (*Give specific praise to each student.*)

Retell

After the group has read the story three times, students should then retell the story in their own words, telling events in the order that they occurred. The format for presenting Retell is as follows:

Now it's time to retell this story.
What did you learn first?
What did you learn next?

Repeat this second question until all major events have been told.

Call on individual students throughout Retell. Guide the process with prompts as necessary, but do NOT supply information. You may need to briefly show a picture on a specific page to help prompt students.

Correcting Errors

Teacher Note: Correct all errors when they occur.

In order for *Teacher-Directed PALS* lessons to have the desired impact of accelerating the reading growth of struggling readers, it is necessary for all errors that occur to be corrected immediately. By correcting all errors as soon as they occur, you ensure that students achieve mastery of all content and that any confusion or misunderstandings are cleared up immediately for the students.

Basic Correction Procedure

Whenever *any* student in the group makes a mistake, the whole group should be corrected using the following TELL, ASK, START AGAIN procedure:

1. TELL the students the correct response. (That letter's sound is /sss/.)

2. ASK the entire group of students for the correct response. (What is this letter's sound?)

3. Back up and repeat the last few items. (Let's back up.)

It is important that you repeat the items in an activity until all of the students can individually respond to all the items, with no errors.

Correcting Specific Errors

Beyond the basic TELL, ASK, START AGAIN correction strategy, there are specific errors that need special correcting techniques.

Stretching Errors

When a student makes an error in stretching a word:

1. Stop as soon as an error occurs. For example, if students are stretching *mom* and a student says /mmm/aaa/, stop the student as soon as you hear the mistake (/aaa/).

2. TELL the correct way to stretch the word ("My turn, /mmm/ooo/mmm/") and emphasize the correct sound. Use the finger cue as you correct.

3. ASK the student to repeat the word correctly. ("Your turn.")

Blending Errors

Sometimes students can stretch a word, but then cannot blend it back into the original word. Typically, when this happens students will leave off a part of the word. For example, after stretching the word *mat*, a student then says the word fast as *at*, leaving off the /m/. If a student makes this kind of error, use the following steps:

1. TELL the correct word, emphasizing the part that was dropped. ("My turn, /mmm/aaa/t/ said fast is *mat*. You left off the /<u>mmm</u>/ in /<u>mmm</u>/a/t/.")

2. Repeat the whole item with the students. ("Let's stretch *mat* together: /mmm/aaa/t/. What word did we stretch? *mat*.")

3. ASK the students to repeat the word by themselves. ("Now stretch *mat* by yourselves.") Pause for answer. "What word did you stretch?" (Pause for answer.)

Misread Words During Passage Reading or Story Sharing

If students read a word incorrectly during Passage Reading or Story Sharing, make your correction depending on what kind of word it is (i.e., either sight words or words that can be sounded out.)

If the missed word can be sounded out, ask the students to sound it out, read it fast, then reread the sentence in which the error occurred. If the students have difficulty sounding out the word, demonstrate for them how to sound out the word and then ask the students to sound it out again, read it fast, then read the entire sentence again.

If the word cannot be sounded out, then tell the students the word, following the TELL, ASK, START AGAIN strategy.

Teaching to Mastery

The key to accelerating reading growth is to hold students to mastery on each Lesson Sheet every day. Mastery means that each student in a group can independently, without your help, complete each task on each Lesson Sheet. Thus, individual turns are the time in which you assess students' mastery levels. If an error occurs during individual practice, this indicates that mastery has not yet been reached for that activity that day, and that reteaching is necessary.

The Lesson Sheets are designed so that that each lesson builds on the last lesson. Thus, it is important that students master each lesson before moving on. If you are following the correction procedure of starting the line or sentence again every time an error happens, mastery should occur.

Mastery Monitoring Form

A Mastery Monitoring Form is provided following the Daily Teaching Format Guides. Copy this form for use with each group of students (see Figure 9). This form serves two purposes:

1. To help you keep track of how students are progressing.
2. To provide feedback to students and to help keep them motivated.

Down the left hand column of the form are the numbers of the lessons, and along the top are the numbers of the Sounds and Words activities for each Lesson Sheet.

Each day, you simply place an X in the box for each activity as the students demonstrate 100% mastery of it. When students master all activities of a lesson, place a sticker, such as a colored dot or star, in the lesson mastery box. Students will enjoy earning these stickers, and you can use the form as a motivational tool.

FIGURE 9
MASTERY MONITORING FORM

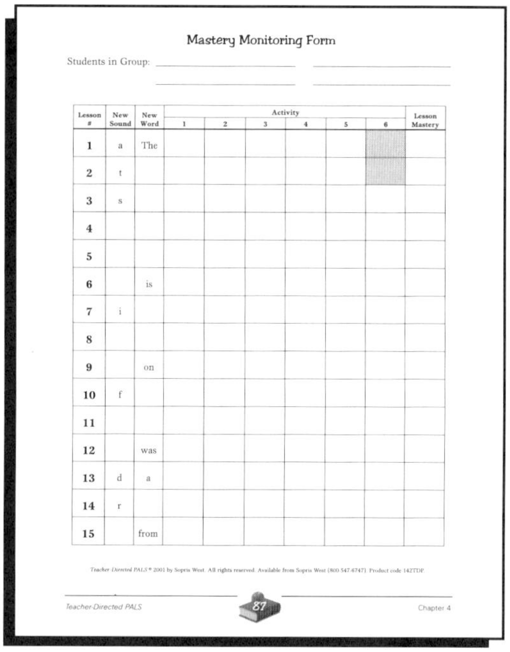

Mastery Monitoring Form

Students in Group: ____________ ____________ ____________ ____________

Lesson #	New Sound	New Word	Activity 1	2	3	4	5	6	Lesson Mastery
1	a	The							
2	t								
3	s								
4									
5									
6		is							
7	i								
8									
9		on							
10	f								
11									
12		was							
13	d	a							
14	r								
15		from							

Teacher-Directed PALS © 2001 by Sopris West. All rights reserved. Available from Sopris West (800-547-6747). Product code 142TDP.

Teacher-Directed PALS 87 Chapter 4

Reteaching for Mastery

Students will not always achieve mastery of a lesson in one session; this is normal. If even one student in a group does not achieve 100% mastery of a section of the lesson, the group should repeat that section at the beginning of the next *Teacher-Directed PALS* session. Once mastery is achieved by *all* students, the award sticker can be affixed.

Daily Teaching Format Guide
for Lessons 1-15

Use the following format each time you present a *Teacher-Directed PALS* lesson numbered 1–15. The format is written for use with two or three students; to adapt it for use with one student, just direct group questions to the individual student.

All students MUST be able to complete each activity independently at 100% accuracy before a lesson is complete.

Have all materials ready before beginning each lesson:

1. Turn to day's Lesson Sheet in this manual

2. Mastery Monitoring Form for this student or group

3. Selected storybook

Sounds and Words Routine

Activity 1: Letter-Sounds

Introducing the New Letter-Sound

Complete this section only if the Lesson Sheet has a new sound presented in the "new sound" box. If there is no new sound, begin the lesson with Cumulative Letter-Sound Review (following).

Review the Sound Pronunciation Guide in Chapter 2 and practice saying the new sound without distortion before presenting it to students.

This is the new sound. *Demonstrate (remember to hum continuous sounds for about two seconds, but say stop sounds quickly).*

Ask group: **What sound?**

Ask each individual student: **What sound?**

Correct and repeat as necessary.

Cumulative Letter-Sound Review

Let's see if you can remember all these sounds. Remember, when I touch a letter you say its sound, and keep saying its sound as long as I touch it.

Place your finger under the first sound and say: **Everybody, what sound?**

Repeat with each letter. Remember to point to continuous sounds for about two seconds, but lift off stop sounds quickly.

Correct and repeat as necessary.

After the group says all of the sounds correctly, say: **Now I'll call on you one at a time.**

In a random order, ask individual students to say three to five sounds. If two or more mistakes occur, make corrections and repeat all the sounds with the group again, then return to individual practice.

Place a check mark on the Mastery Monitoring Form for this activity of the lesson.

Activity 2: Hearing Sounds

Remember to use the finger cue to control the students' pacing of each word for this activity. Students should hold continuous sounds for about two seconds, but say stop sounds quickly. There should be no pauses between sounds when stretching. Be sure to hold your Manual so that children are not looking at these words.

Students should not see your list of words during this activity, as this is an auditory activity.

Now we're going to listen for the sounds we hear inside words. First you will stretch a word, then you will say it fast. Remember, when you stretch a word you will say each sound that you hear in the word, holding up one finger for each sound.

Everybody, hold up your fist like this. *Model for students.*

First word. *(Insert from Lesson Sheet.)* **Stretch.** *(Insert from Lesson Sheet.)*

Hold up one finger for each sound, but do NOT say the sound yourself. Students should not say the next sound until you hold up the next finger.

What word did you stretch? *(Wait for students to answer.)* **Yes,** *(insert from Lesson Sheet).*

Next word.

Repeat the process with each word listed on the Lesson Sheet for Activity 2. Correct and repeat as necessary.

After the group stretches all the words correctly, say: **Now I'll call on you one at a time.**

Each student should segment and blend two to three words with 100% accuracy.

Place a check mark on the Mastery Monitoring Form for this activity of the lesson.

Activity 3: More Letter-Sound Practice

We're going to practice saying the sounds of letters again. Show me how well you can say the sound for each of these letters. *Point to first sound and say:* **Everybody, what sound?**

Repeat with each letter. Remember to point to continuous sounds for about two seconds, but lift off stop sounds quickly.

Correct and repeat as necessary.

After the group says all of the sounds correctly, say: **Now I'll call on you one at a time.**

In a random order, ask individual students to say three to five sounds. If two or more mistakes occur, make corrections and repeat all the sounds with the group again, then return to individual practice.

Place a check mark on the Mastery Monitoring Form for this activity of the lesson.

Activity 4: Sounding Out

Now you're going to sound out words, then you'll read them. When I touch the dot under a letter, you say its sound and keep saying its sound until I touch the dot under the next letter. You will not stop between sounds; you will hum the word.

Place your fingertip beside the first word.

Sound it out.

Slide your finger under each letter, pointing to each dot in turn. Point to continuous sounds for about two seconds, but move off of stop sounds quickly. There should be no pauses between sounds when sounding out.

Correct and repeat as necessary.

Read it.

Repeat for each word.

After the group sounds out all of the words correctly, say: **Now I'll call on you one at a time.**

In a random order, ask individual students to sound out and then read one or two words. If two or more mistakes occur, make corrections and repeat all the words with the group again, then return to individual practice.

Place a check mark on the Mastery Monitoring Form for this activity of the lesson.

Activity 5: Sight Word Reading

The New Word

Complete this section only if the Lesson Sheet you are working on has a new sight word presented in the "new word" box. If there is no new word, go to Cumulative Sight Word Review (following).

Point to the new sight word and say: **We have a new word to learn to read today.**

This word is *(insert from Lesson Sheet).* **What's this word?** *(Wait for students to answer.)*

Yes, *(insert from Lesson Sheet).*

Ask each individual student: **What's this word?**

Correct and repeat as necessary.

Cumulative Sight Word Review

Now let's read the other words. When I point to a word you read it.

Point to each sight word and ask: **What's this word?**

Repeat for each word.

After the group reads all of the words correctly, say: **Now I'll call on you one at a time.**

In a random order, ask individual students to read several words.

If two or more mistakes occur, make corrections and repeat all the words with the group again, then return to individual practice.

Place a check mark on the Mastery Monitoring Form for this activity of the lesson.

___

Activity 6: Passage Reading

___

Now we're ready to read the story. When I point to a word you'll sound it out together, then read it fast. If it's a sight word, you'll just read it fast.

Point to the first word of the first sentence.

Sound it out.

Slide your finger under each letter, pointing to continuous sounds for about two seconds, but moving off of stop sounds quickly. There should be no pauses between sounds when sounding out.

Correct and repeat as necessary.

Read it. *(Or, if the word is a sight word, say:* **You know this word. Read it.***)*

Sound out and read the entire story in unison. Remind students to wait until you point to a word.

Now I'll call on you one at a time. *Ask individual students to sound out and read two or three sentences independently. Correct and repeat as necessary.*

Place a check mark on the Mastery Monitoring Form for this activity of the lesson.

Verbally praise students and give them a sticker or other reward for attaining mastery. Put the Lesson Sheet away and get out the day's storybook.

___

Story Sharing Routine

Activity 7: Pretend-Read

Hold up the storybook so that all students in the group can see the cover.

Here's today's story. The title of this book is _____. *(Point to each word of the title as you read it.)* **It was written by _____.** **Now let's Pretend-Read this book. Remember that when we Pretend-Read a book, we look at the pictures and predict what we think the book is about.**

Turn to the starting page. Turn the book so that the students can see the pictures, and say: **Look at the pictures. What do you think is happening on these pages?** *Call on one student to answer.*

Quickly repeat this process on each page. Remember, Pretend-Reading should require no more than one to two minutes. Prompt students to attend to specific information in the pictures as necessary.

If students do not state a prediction as a complete sentence, model how to "say the whole sentence," and ask students to repeat the whole sentence.

Activity 8: Read Aloud

Step 1—Echo Read:

Now let's read this book. As we read it, check to see if any of your predictions about what happens in the story were right. We'll read this story several times. The first time I'll read a sentence, then you'll read the same sentence. Listen carefully and look at each word as I read it.

Turn back to the starting page and turn the book so that the students can see the text. Read the first sentence, pointing to each word as you read it, then say:

Your turn.

Guide students by pointing to each word as they read. If an error occurs, tell them the word and repeat the sentence.

Repeat this process through entire book.

Did any of your predictions come true? *Point out one or two that came true.*

Step 2—Choral Reading:

Now let's read the book again. This time we'll read the book together.

Read each sentence of the book in unison with the students. Read fairly slowly, and keep your voice low so that the students are leading. If students are trailing behind, slow down your reading rate.

Step 3—Independent Reading:

Now I'll call on you one at a time to read some of this story.

Ask each student to read a few sentences from the book aloud. If an error occurs, tell the student the word and ask him or her to reread the sentence. If the same student makes another error, tell the student the word and reread the sentence yourself, then ask the student to reread the sentence.

Excellent reading, everyone. *(Give specific praise to each student.)*

Activity 9: Retell

Now it's time to retell this story. What did you learn first?

What did you learn next?

Repeat this second question until all major events have been told.

Call on individual students throughout Retell. Guide the process with prompts as necessary, but do NOT supply information. You may need to briefly show a picture on a specific page to help prompt students.

Daily Teaching Format Guide
for Lessons 16-36

Use the following format each time you present a *Teacher-Directed PALS* lesson numbered 16–36. The format is written for use with two or three students; to adapt it for use with one student, just direct group questions to the individual student.

All students MUST be able to complete each activity independently at 100% accuracy before a lesson is complete.

Have all materials ready before beginning each lesson:

1. Turn to day's Lesson Sheet in this manual

2. Mastery Monitoring Form for this student or group

3. Selected storybook

Sounds and Words Routine

Activity 1: Letter-Sounds

Introducing the New Letter-Sound

Complete this section only if the Lesson Sheet has a new sound presented in the "new sound" box. If there is no new sound, begin the lesson with Cumulative Letter-Sound Review (following).

Review the Sound Pronunciation Guide in Chapter 2 and practice saying the new sound without distortion before presenting it to students.

This is the new sound. *Demonstrate (remember to hum continuous sounds for about two seconds, but say stop sounds quickly).*

Ask group: **What sound?**

Ask each individual student: **What sound?**

Correct and repeat as necessary.

Cumulative Letter-Sound Review

Let's see if you can remember all these sounds. Remember, when I touch a letter you say its sound, and keep saying its sound as long as I touch it.

Place your finger under the first sound and say: **Everybody, what sound?**

Repeat with each letter. Remember to point to continuous sounds for about two seconds, but lift off stop sounds quickly.

Correct and repeat as necessary.

After the group says all of the sounds correctly, say: **Now I'll call on you one at a time.**

In a random order, ask individual students to say three to five sounds. If two or more mistakes occur, make corrections and repeat all the sounds with the group again, then return to individual practice.

Place a check mark on the Mastery Monitoring Form for this activity of the lesson.

Activity 2: Hearing Sounds

Remember to use the finger cue to control the students' pacing of each word for this activity. Students should hold continuous sounds for about two seconds, but say stop sounds quickly. There should be no pauses between sounds when stretching.

Students should not see your list of words during this activity as this is an auditory activity.

Now we're going to listen for the sounds we hear inside words. First you will stretch a word, then you will say it fast. Remember, when you stretch a word you will say each sound that you hear in the word, holding up one finger for each sound.

Everybody, hold up your fist like this. *Model for students.*

First word. *(Insert from Lesson Sheet.)* **Stretch.** *(Insert from Lesson Sheet.)*

Hold up one finger for each sound, but do NOT say the sound yourself. Students should not say the next sound until you hold up the next finger.

What word did you stretch? *(Wait for students to answer.)* **Yes,** *(insert from Lesson Sheet).*

Next word.

Repeat the process with each word listed on the Lesson Sheet for Activity 2. Correct and repeat as necessary.

After the group stretches all the words correctly, say: **Now I'll call on you one at a time.**

Each student should segment and blend two to three words with 100% accuracy.

Place a check mark on the Mastery Monitoring Form for this activity of the lesson.

Activity 3: More Letter-Sound Practice

We're going to practice saying the sounds of letters again. Show me how well you can say the sound for each of these letters. *Point to the first sound and say:* **Everybody, what sound?**

Repeat with each letter. Remember to point to continuous sounds for about two seconds, but lift off stop sounds quickly.

Correct and repeat as necessary.

After the group says all of the sounds correctly, say: **Now I'll call on you one at a time.**

In a random order, ask individual students to say three to five sounds. If two or more mistakes occur, make corrections and repeat all the sounds with the group again, then return to individual practice.

Place a check mark on the Mastery Monitoring Form for this activity of the lesson.

Activity 4: Sounding Out

Sounding Out Words, Then Reading Them

Now you're going to sound out words, then you'll read them. When I touch the dot under a letter, you say its sound and keep saying its sound until I touch the dot under the next letter. You will not stop between sounds; you will hum the word.

Place your fingertip beside the first word.

Sound it out.

Slide your finger under each letter, pointing to each dot in turn. Point to continuous sounds for about two seconds, but move off of stop sounds quickly. There should be no pauses between sounds when sounding out.

Correct and repeat as necessary.

Read it.

Repeat for each word.

Reading the Words Fast

Good sounding out. Now let's read these words fast.

Point to the first word.

When I tap next to a word, you tell me the word. I'll give you think time, so wait for me to tap.

First word. *(Think time should be one to three seconds, depending on students' ability.)*

What word? *(Tap. Wait for students to answer.)*

Point to the next word. **Next word.**

Repeat with entire list.

In a random order, ask individuals to read several words fast. If an error occurs, return to sounding out and saying the word fast, then return to individual practice. If more than two errors occur, repeat sounding out format with the entire group before continuing to read the words fast.

Activity 5: Sight Word Reading

The New Word

Complete this section only if the Lesson Sheet you are working on has a new sight word presented in the "new word" box. If there is no new word, go to Cumulative Sight Word Review (following).

Point to the new sight word and say: **We have a new word to learn to read today.**

This word is *(insert from Lesson Sheet).* **What's this word?** *(Wait for students to answer.)*

Yes, *(insert from Lesson Sheet).*

Ask each individual student: **What's this word?**

Correct and repeat as necessary.

Cumulative Sight Word Review

Now let's read the other words. When I point to a word you read it.

Point to each sight word and ask: **What's this word?**

Repeat for each word.

After the group reads all of the words correctly, say: **Now I'll call on you one at a time.**

In a random order, ask individual students to read several words.

If two or more mistakes occur, make corrections and repeat all the words with the group again, then return to individual practice.

Place a check mark on the Mastery Monitoring Form for this activity of the lesson.

Activity 6: Passage Reading

Now we're ready to read the story. When I point to a word you'll sound it out together, then read it fast. If it's a sight word, you'll just read it fast.

Point to the first word of the first sentence.

Sound it out.

Slide your finger under each letter, pointing to continuous sounds for about two seconds, but moving off of stop sounds quickly. There should be no pauses between sounds when sounding out.

Correct and repeat as necessary.

Read it. *(Or, if the word is a sight word, say:* **You know this word. Read it.***)*

Sound out and read the entire story in unison. Remind students to wait until you point to a word.

Now I'll call on you one at a time. *Ask individual students to sound out and read two or three sentences independently. Correct and repeat as necessary.*

Place a check mark on the Mastery Monitoring Form for this activity of the lesson.

Verbally praise students and give them a sticker or other reward for attaining mastery. Put the Lesson Sheet away and get out the day's storybook.

Story Sharing Routine

Activity 7: Pretend-Read

Hold up the storybook so that all students in the group can see the cover.

Here's today's story. The title of this book is _____. *(Point to each word of the title as you read it.)* **It was written by _____.** **Now let's Pretend-Read this book. Remember that when we Pretend-Read a book, we look at the pictures and predict what we think the book is about.**

Turn to the starting page. Turn the book so that the students can see the pictures, and say: **Look at the pictures. What do you think is happening on these pages?** *Call on one student to answer.*

Quickly repeat this process on each page. Remember, Pretend-Reading should require no more than one to two minutes. Prompt students to attend to specific information in the pictures as necessary.

If students do not state a prediction as a complete sentence, model how to "say the whole sentence," and ask students to repeat the whole sentence.

Activity 8: Read Aloud

Step 1—Echo Read:

Now let's read this book. As we read it, check to see if any of your predictions about what happens in the story were right. We'll read this story several times. The first time I'll read a sentence, then you'll read the same sentence. Listen carefully and look at each word as I read it.

Turn back to the starting page and turn the book so that the students can see the text. Read the first sentence, pointing to each word as you read it, then say:

Your turn.

Guide students by pointing to each word as they read. If an error occurs, tell them the word and repeat the sentence.

Repeat this process through entire book.

Did any of your predictions come true? *Point out one or two that came true.*

Step 2—Choral Reading:

Now let's read the book again. This time we'll read the book together.

Read each sentence of the book in unison with the students. Read fairly slowly, and keep your voice low so that the students are leading. If students are trailing behind, slow down your reading rate.

Step 3—Independent Reading:

Now I'll call on you one at a time to read some of this story.

Ask each student to read a few sentences from the book aloud. If an error occurs, tell the student the word and ask him or her to reread the sentence. If the same student makes another error, tell the student the word and reread the sentence yourself, then ask the student to reread the sentence.

Excellent reading, everyone. *(Give specific praise to each student.)*

Activity 9: Retell

Now it's time to retell this story. What did you learn first?

What did you learn next?

Repeat this second question until all major events have been told.

Call on individual students throughout Retell. Guide the process with prompts as necessary, but do NOT supply information. You may need to briefly show a picture on a specific page to help prompt students.

Daily Teaching Format Guide
for Lessons 37-57

Use the following format each time you present a *Teacher-Directed PALS* lesson numbered 37–57. The format is written for use with two or three students; to adapt it for use with one student, just direct group questions to the individual student.

All students MUST be able to complete each activity at 100% accuracy before a lesson is complete.

Have all materials ready before beginning each lesson:

1. Turn to day's Lesson Sheet in this manual

2. Mastery Monitoring Form for this student or group

3. Selected storybook

Sounds and Words Routine

Activity 1: Letter-Sounds

Introducing the New Letter-Sound

Complete this section only if the Lesson Sheet has a new sound presented in the "new sound" box. If there is no new sound, begin the lesson with Cumulative Letter-Sound Review (following).

Review the Sound Pronunciation Guide in Chapter 2 and practice saying the new sound without distortion before presenting it to students.

This is the new sound. *Demonstrate (remember to hum continuous sounds for about two seconds, but say stop sounds quickly).*

Ask group: **What sound?**

Ask each individual student: **What sound?**

Correct and repeat as necessary.

Cumulative Letter-Sound Review

Let's see if you can remember all these sounds. Remember, when I touch a letter you say its sound, and keep saying its sound as long as I touch it.

Place your finger under the first sound and say: **Everybody, what sound?**

Repeat with each letter. Remember to point to continuous sounds for about two seconds, but lift off stop sounds quickly.

Correct and repeat as necessary.

After the group says all of the sounds correctly, say: **Now I'll call on you one at a time.**

In a random order, ask individual students to say three to five sounds. If two or more mistakes occur, make corrections and repeat all the sounds with the group again, then return to individual practice.

Place a check mark on the Mastery Monitoring Form for this activity of the lesson.

Activity 2: Sounding Out

Sounding Out Words, Then Reading Them

Now you're going to sound out words, then you'll read them. When I touch the dot under a letter, you say its sound and keep saying its sound until I touch the dot under the next letter. You will not stop between sounds; you will hum the word.

Place your fingertip beside the first word.

Sound it out.

Slide your finger under each letter, pointing to each dot in turn. Point to continuous sounds for about two seconds, but move off of stop sounds quickly. There should be no pauses between sounds when sounding out.

Correct and repeat as necessary.

Read it.

Repeat for each word.

Reading the Words Fast

Now we're going to read words in chunks, then we'll read them fast. Small words have only one chunk, so you'll read them fast first. For big words, you'll read each underlined chunk, then you'll read the whole word fast. When I touch an underlined part you'll read it. After you read each underlined part, you'll read the whole word fast.

(Point to the first word.) **First word.** *(Point to the first underlined part, and allow students one to two seconds of think time, as necessary.)* **Read the part.** *(Repeat with each additional underlined part.)*

Now, read the word. *(Quickly move your finger from left to right under the word.)*

Next word.

(Repeat procedure with remaining words. If an error occurs in reading a chunk, sound out the chunk and then return to reading each chunk fast.)

Good chunking. Now let's read these words fast.

Point to the first word.

When I tap on a word, you tell me the word. I'll give you think time, so wait for me to tap.

First word. *(Allow think time of one half to two seconds, depending on students' ability.)* **What word?** *(Tap.)*

Point to the next word.

Next word. *(Tap.)*

Repeat with entire list. In a random order, ask individuals to read several words the fast way. If an error occurs, return to the process of first chunking and then saying the word fast. If necessary, sound out a chunk, then return to individual practice. If more than two errors occur, repeat chunking format with entire group before continuing to read the words fast.

Activity 3: Sight Word Reading

The New Word

Complete this section only if the Lesson Sheet you are working on has a new sight word presented in the "new word" box. If there is no new word, go to Cumulative Sight Word Review (following).

Point to the new sight word and say: **We have a new word to learn to read today.**

This word is *(insert from Lesson Sheet).* **What's this word?** *(Wait for students to answer.)*

Yes, *(insert from Lesson Sheet).*

Ask each individual student: **What's this word?**

Correct and repeat as necessary.

Cumulative Sight Word Review

Now let's read the other words. When I point to a word you read it.

Point to each sight word and ask: **What's this word?**

Repeat for each word.

After the group reads all of the words correctly, say: **Now I'll call on you one at a time.**

In a random order, ask individual students to read several words.

If two or more mistakes occur, make corrections and repeat all the words with the group again, then return to individual practice.

Place a check mark on the Mastery Monitoring Form for this activity of the lesson.

Activity 4: Passage Reading

Now we're ready to read the story. When I point to a word you'll read it together. If you miss a word, we'll sound it out, then read it fast. We'll then read the sentence again.

First word.

Point to the first word. Allow think time of one to three seconds, depending on students' ability. Then lift your finger and move it to the next word. Wait the appropriate think time and move to the next word.

Read entire story in unison fashion, pointing to each word. If students do not read together, remind them to wait until you point to a word. After reading the entire story together, ask individual students to read sentences independently.

Verbally praise students and give them a sticker or other reward for attaining mastery. Put the Lesson Sheet away and get out the day's storybook.

Story Sharing Routine

Activity 5: Pretend-Read

Hold up the storybook so that all students in the group can see the cover.

Here's today's story. The title of this book is _____. *(Point to each word of the title as you read it.)* **It was written by _____.** **Now let's Pretend-Read this book. Remember that when we Pretend-Read a book, we look at the pictures and predict what we think the book is about.**

Turn to the starting page. Turn the book so that the students can see the pictures, and say: **Look at the pictures. What do you think is happening on these pages?** *Call on one student to answer.*

Quickly repeat this process on each page. Remember, Pretend-Reading should require no more than one to two minutes. Prompt students to attend to specific information in the pictures as necessary.

If students do not state a prediction as a complete sentence, model how to "say the whole sentence," and ask students to repeat the whole sentence.

Activity 6: Read Aloud

Step 1—Echo Read:

Now let's read this book. As we read it, check to see if any of your predictions about what happens in the story were right. We'll read this story several times. The first time I'll read a sentence, then you'll read the same sentence. Listen carefully and look at each word as I read it.

Turn back to the starting page and turn the book so that the students can see the text. Read the first sentence, pointing to each word as you read it, then say:

Your turn.

Guide students by pointing to each word as they read. If an error occurs, tell them the word and repeat the sentence.

Repeat this process through entire book.

Did any of your predictions come true? *Point out one or two that came true.*

Step 2—Choral Reading:

Now let's read the book again. This time we'll read the book together.

Read each sentence of the book in unison with the students. Read fairly slowly, and keep your voice low so that the students are leading. If students are trailing behind, slow down your reading rate.

Step 3—Independent Reading:

Now I'll call on you one at a time to read some of this story.

Ask each student to read a few sentences from the book aloud. If an error occurs, tell the student the word and ask him or her to reread the sentence. If the same student makes another error, tell the student the word and reread the sentence yourself, then ask the student to reread the sentence.

Excellent reading, everyone. *(Give specific praise to each student.)*

Activity 7: Retell

Now it's time to retell this story. What did you learn first?

What did you learn next?

Repeat this second question until all major events have been told.

Call on individual students throughout Retell. Guide the process with prompts as necessary, but do NOT supply information. You may need to briefly show a picture on a specific page to help prompt students.

Mastery Monitoring Form

Students in Group: _____   _____

_____   _____

Lesson #	New Sound	New Word	Activity 1	2	3	4	5	6	Lesson Mastery
1	a	The							
2	t								
3	s								
4									
5									
6		is							
7	i								
8									
9		on							
10	f								
11									
12		was							
13	d	a							
14	r								
15		from							

Mastery Monitoring Form (continued)

Lesson #	New Sound	New Word	Activity 1	Activity 2	Activity 3	Activity 4	Activity 5	Activity 6	Lesson Mastery
16	o	with							
17	g								
18									
19									
20	h								
21									
22	c	has							
23									
24	l								
25	e	because							
26									
27	n	he							
28	b								
29									
30	w	to							
31	p	are							
32									

Mastery Monitoring Form (continued)

Lesson #	New Sound	New Word	Activity						Lesson Mastery
			1	2	3	4	5	6	
33	ing	she							
34	ch	they							
35									
36	u	have							

Starting at Lesson 37: (1) The Hearing Sounds activity is removed, (2) Letter-Sounds occurs only one time, and Sounding Out is done by syllable rather than by letter. For these lessons use the Daily Teaching Format Guide for Lessons 37-57.

Lesson #	New Sound	New Word	Activity				Lesson Mastery
			1	2	3	4	
37	er	than					
38							
39	j	his					
40	k	of					
41	ck						
42		look					
43	ee	their					
44	ea						
45		I					
46	sh	for					

Mastery Monitoring Form (continued)

Lesson #	New Sound	New Word	Activity				Lesson Mastery
			1	2	3	4	
47	aw	over					
48							
49	ur	As, when					
50	ir	said					
51							
52	th	your					
53	ou	my, too					
54							
55	ow	were					
56	ar						
57		you					

References

Brown, I. S., and R. H. Felton. 1990. Effects of instruction on beginning reading skills in children at risk for reading disability. *Reading and Writing: An Interdisciplinary Journal* 2: 223-241.

Carnine, D., J. Silbert, and E. J. Kameenui. 1997. *Direct instruction reading.* Columbus, OH: Merrill.

Chall, J. S. 1989. Learning to read: The great debate 20 years later. *Phi Delta Kappan* 70 (7): 521-538.

Chard, D. J., D. C. Simmons, and E. J. Kameenui. 1995. *Understanding the role of word recognition in reading and the reading process: Synthesis of research on beginning reading.* Eugene: National Center to Improve the Tools of Educators, University of Oregon. Report No. 15.

Daneman, M. 1991. Individual differences in reading skills. In *Handbook of reading research: Volume 2*, (512-538). Edited by R. Barr, M. L. Kamil, P. B. Mosenthal, and P. D. Pearson. New York: Longman.

Ehri, L. C. 1998. Grapheme-phoneme knowledge is essential for learning to read words in English. In *Word recognition in beginning reading.* Edited by J. Metsala and L. Ehri. Hillsdale, NJ: Lawrence Erlbaum Assoc.

Flood, J., and D. Lapp. 1991. Reading comprehension instruction. In *Handbook of research on teaching the English language arts* (732-742). Edited by J. Flood, J. M. Jensen, D. Lapp, and J. R. Squire. New York: McMillan.

Foorman, B. R. 1995. Research on "the great debate": Code-oriented versus whole language approaches to reading instruction. *School Psychology Review* 24: 376-392.

Foorman, B. R., D. J. Francis, J. M. Fletcher, C. Schatschneider, and P. Mehta. 1998. The role of instruction in learning to read: Preventing reading failure in at-risk children. *Journal of Educational Psychology* 90: 37-55.

Foorman, B. R., D. J. Francis, S. E. Shaywitz, B. A. Shaywitz, and J. M. Fletcher. 1997. The case for early reading interventions. In *Foundations of reading acquisition and dyslexia: Implications for early intervention* (243-264). Edited by B. A. Blachman. Mahwah, NJ: Erlbaum Associates.

Foorman, B. R., D. J. Francis, D. Winikates, P. D. Mehta, C. Schatschneider, and J. M. Fletcher. 1997. Early intervention for children with reading disabilities. *Scientific Studies of Reading* 1(3): 255-276.

Fountas, I. C., and G. S. Pinnell. 1996. *Guided reading: Good first teaching for all children.* Portsmouth, NH: Heinemann.

Galda, L., and B. E. Cullinan. 1991. Literature for literacy: What research says about the benefits of using trade books in the classroom. In *Handbook of research on teaching the English language arts* (529-535). Edited by J. Flood, J. M. Jensen, D. Lapp, and J. R. Squire. New York: McMillan.

Langenberg, D. N., and associates. 2000. *Report of the National Reading Panel: Teaching children to read: An evidenced-based assessment of the scientific literature on reading and its implications for reading instruction: Reports of the subgroups.* Bethesda, MD: National Institute of Child Health and Human Development, National Institutes of Health.

Mathes, P. G., and A. E. Babyak. (In press). The effects of peer-assisted learning strategies for first-grade readers with and without additional mini-skills lessons. *Learning Disabilities Research and Practice.*

Mathes, P. G., and J. K. Torgesen. 1998. All children can learn to read: Critical care for students with special needs. *Peabody Journal of Education* 73: 317-340.

Mathes, P. G., J. K. Torgesen, and J. C. Menchetti. 2000. An examination of instructional delivery arrangements in teaching reading to struggling first-grade readers.

Mathes, P. G., J. K. Torgesen, and S. H. Allen. 2000. *Peer Assisted Literacy Strategies for First-Grade Readers.* Longmont, CO: Sopris West.

Martinez, M., and N. Roser. 1985. Read it again: The value of repeated readings during story time. *The Reading Teacher* 38: 782-786.

National Research Council. 1998. *Preventing reading difficulties in young children.* Washington DC: National Academy Press.

Rashotte, C. A., and J. K. Torgesen. 1985. Repeated reading and reading fluency in learning disabled children. *Reading Research Quarterly* 20: 180-188.

Share, D. L. 1995. Phonological recoding and self-teaching: Sine qua non of reading acquisition. *Cognition* 55: 151-218.

Share, D. L., and K. E. Stanovich. 1995. Cognitive processes in early reading development: A model of acquisition and individual differences. *Issues in Education: Contributions From Educational Psychology* 1: 1-57.

Sindelar, P. T., L. Monda, and L. O'Shea. 1990. Effects of repeated readings on instructional- and mastery-level readers. *Journal of Educational Research* 83: 220-226.

Snow, C. E., M. S. Burns, and P. Griffin. 1998. *Preventing reading difficulties in young children.* Washington, DC: National Academy Press.

Stanovich, K. E. 1991. Word recognition: Changing perspectives. In *Handbook of reading research: Volume 2* (418-452). Edited by R. Barr, M. Kamil, P. Mosenthal, and P. D. Pearson. White Plains, NY: Longman.

Torgesen, J. K. 1997. The prevention and remediation of reading disabilities: Evaluating what we know from research. *Journal of Academic Language Therapy* 1: 11-47.

———1998. Instructional interventions for children with reading Disabilities. In *Specific Reading Disability: A View of the Spectrum* (157-182). Edited by B. K. Shapiro, P. J. Accardo, and A. J. Capute. Parkton, MD: York Press.

Torgesen, J. K, and P. G. Mathes. 2000. *A basic guide to understanding, assessing, and teaching phonological awareness.* Austin, TX: Pro-Ed.

Torgesen, J. K., R. K. Wagner, and C. A. Rashotte. 1997. The prevention and remediation of severe reading disabilities: Keeping the end in mind. *Scientific Studies of Reading,* 1: 217-234.

Torgesen, J. K., R. K. Wagner, and C. A. Rashotte, A. W. Alexander, and T. Conway. 1997. Preventive and remedial interventions for children with severe reading disabilities. *Learning Disabilities: A Multidisciplinary Journal* 8(1): 51-61.

Vellutino, F. R. 1991. Introduction to three studies of reading acquisition: Convergent findings on theoretical foundations of code-based versus whole-language approaches to reading instruction. *Journal of Educational Psychology* 83: 437-443.

Vellutino, F. R., D. M. Scanlon, E. R. Sipay, S. G. Small, A. Pratt, R. Chen, and M. B. Denckla. 1996. Cognitive profiles of difficult-to-remediate and readily remediated poor readers: Early intervention as a vehicle for distinguishing between cognitive and experiential deficits as basic causes of specific reading disability. *Journal of Educational Psychology* 88: 601-638.

Weinstein, G., and N. L. Cooke. 1992. The effects of two repeated reading interventions on generalization of fluency. *Learning Disability Quarterly* 15: 21-28.

Lesson Sheets 1-57

Lesson Sheet 1 (page 1)

a

m   a   m   a   m

t   a   m   t   a

at   am   mat
(2)   (2)   (3)

m   a   t   a   t

a   t   m   a   m

Lesson Sheet 1 (page 2)

at

the

Lesson Sheet 2 (page 1)

T

a T m t T a

m a T m t a

mat   am   at
(3)   (2)   (2)

T t a m a T

m a t a T m

a̤t

the

Lesson Sheet 3 (page 1)

s

| T | s | a | m | s | m |

| t | a | s | T | m | a |

am	it	sat	sit	mat
(2)	(2)	(3)	(3)	(3)

| s | a | t | m | s | a |

| m | s | a | t | m | s |

The   the

The

Sam sat at the mat.

Lesson Sheet 4 (page 1)

s a s a m T

m t s a t s

am	Sam	mitt	sad	it	at
(2)	(3)	(3)	(3)	(2)	(2)

T s a m s m

t a s T m a

at   Sam

mat   am

The

The mat

Sam sat.

Lesson Sheet 5 (page 1)

t m t a t a m

t s a s m t s

am	it	Sam	sit	fit	fat
(2)	(2)	(3)	(3)	(3)	(3)

s a s a m T s

m t s a t s T

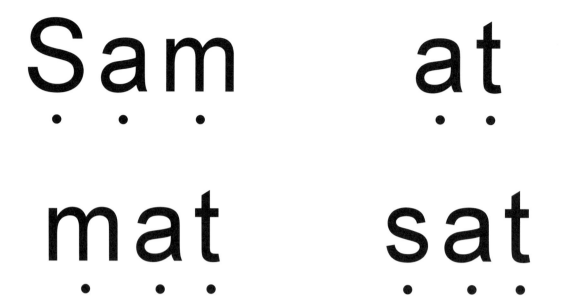

Sam   at

mat   sat

the   The

Sam sat at the mat.

Lesson Sheet 6 (page 1)

s a s m t s a

m T s m a t m

am   sit   sat   fit   sad   mat
(2)   (3)   (3)   (3)   (3)   (3)

t m t a t a m

t s a s m t s

Sam   am

mat   at

sat

is   the   is

Sam sat at the mat.

Lesson Sheet 7 (page 1)

i

s i m t i s a

t m i t m s i

it	sad	mat	mad	sit	and	ram
(2)	(3)	(3)	(3)	(3)	(3)	(3)

s i s m t i a

m T s i a t i

at am

mat sit

Sam

the   is

Sam is at the mat.

Sam sat at the mat.

Lesson Sheet 8 _(page 1)

i s m i t s

a m a s i m

fit	fat	rat	rid	sat	Sam
(3)	(3)	(3)	(3)	(3)	(3)

i s i m t i s a

t m i t m s i m

am   at

it   sit

Sam

the   is

Sam, sit.

Sam sat.

Sam is at the mat.

Lesson Sheet 9 (page 1)

i a m s i t

a m a i a t

fin	fan	ran	run	if	Sam's	sit	sits
(3)	(3)	(3)	(3)	(2)	(4)	(3)	(4)

i s m i t s a

m a s i m a t

Activity 4

it its

at sit

mit Sam

Activity 5

on the is

on

Sam is on the mat.

Sam sat on the mat.

Lesson Sheet 10 (page 1)

f

i f a i f m s

i f a s t i f m

rot	rim	fan	fit	fat	if	it	at	sit
(3)	(3)	(3)	(3)	(3)	(2)	(2)	(2)	(3)

i f a m f s i t

f a m f s i a f

at   Sam

it   its

sit   sits

on   the   is

Sam sits on the mat.

Sam is on the mat.

Lesson Sheet 11 (page 1)

a m f i s T

F a t s i f a i

Sam's	mad	fat	if	fit	mitt	rag	hot	rot
(4)	(3)	(3)	(2)	(3)	(3)	(3)	(3)	(3)

f i f a i f m s

i f a s t i f m

it   mat

fit   fat

sits   sit

is   on   the

Sam is fat.

Fat Sam sat on the mat.

Fat Sam sits.

Lesson Sheet 12 (page 1)

a m i a T f m

s F t i a t T

Tim's	mitt	fits	dad	mad	tip
(4)	(3)	(4)	(3)	(3)	(3)

f a m f i s T f

F a t s i f a i

Lesson Sheet 12 (page 2)

mitt   fat

Sam   am

mad   mid

fit   Sam's

Activity 5

| was | on | the |

was   is

The mitt was Sam's.

Sam's mitt was on the mat.

The mitt fit Sam.

Lesson Sheet 13 (page 1)

d	D

f   d   i   a   m   d   F

t   s   D   d   m   i

dad	ham	fit	Sam's	dim	ram	rat	hat	mom
(3)	(3)	(3)	(4)	(3)	(3)	(3)	(3)	(3)

a   d   m   i   a   T   d

d   s   F   t   d   i   a

Activity 4

mat   mitt

fit   dad

Sam's   its

it   dim

Activity 5

[a]   was   on   is

a   the

Dad was hot.

Sam is fit.

Sam's mitt fit Dad.

Dad was at the mat.

Lesson Sheet 14 (page 1)

r

d r a T r d i

D r s i F d r

rat	dad	did	rim	ram	Tim	Tad	rid	had
(3)	(3)	(3)	(3)	(3)	(3)	(3)	(3)	(3)

d D f d a m d t

s d m i s F d

dad   rim

sad   dad

rat   did

fit   mad

was   is   on   the

a

Sam the rat was fat.

Sam the rat was sad.

Sam's dad was mad.

Dad was mad at Sam the fat rat.

Lesson Sheet 15 (page 1)

r d f i a r f

a s r t m i

its	fan	mom	man	Tad	did	Sam's	dad's	rat
(3)	(3)	(3)	(3)	(3)	(3)	(4)	(4)	(3)

d a T r d m

i D r s i t

fat   dad

rid   Sam's

Dad   ram

Sid   did

from   was   is

the   a

Sam is a rat.

Sid is a ram.

Sam sat on Sid.

Sid is mad at Sam.

Sam is sad.

Lesson Sheet 16 (page 1)

o

r o t a m s

f a d i r o

rot	fan	rim	Tom	Dads	mid	rod	fin	hat
(3)	(3)	(3)	(3)	(4)	(3)	(3)	(3)	(3)

r d f o r D

s t a m i r

Mom   Dad

did   mats

Tom   rats

mid   rot

with   on   the

a   on   from

Sam is mad at Tom.

Sam's mom is with Tom.

Tom is Sid's dad.

Sam's mom sits with Sid's dad.

Lesson Sheet 17 (page 1)

g

g s m T g f

t f g a t r

rat	dad	Tom	raft	grass	dog	fig
(3)	(3)	(3)	(4)	(4)	(3)	(3)

g t s g o i

m d i r T s

dog	got
mom	tag
mad	fat
ram	fit

a   with   the

Sam got a dog.

Sam's dog was fat.

The dog sat with Sam.

Sam got the dog a dog tag.

Lesson Sheet 18 (page 1)

g   o   r   d   o   f   s

r   i   m   t   a   g   o

got	Tom	rag	dad	sad	rods	mom	rat	it's
(3)	(3)	(3)	(3)	(3)	(4)	(3)	(3)	(3)

fat	Tim	fig
(3)	(3)	(3)

o   f   d   s   i   g   r

g   r   a   T   m   f

tag   sit

dog   ram

rats   got

did   tags

is   from   with

The dog is with Sam on the mat.

A dog tag was on the mat.

Sam's dog got the tag.

The dog was glad.

Lesson Sheet 19 (page 1)

---

d o g r i t f

t m o r a g

---

mom's	sits	dim	grass	off	raft	soft	tags	dig
(4)	(4)	(3)	(4)	(2)	(4)	(4)	(4)	(3)

---

d g s o i r

f r a g t m

mats	dig
• • • •	• • •
raft	rat
• • • •	• • •
dot	soft
• • •	• • • •
digs	fits
• • • •	• • • •

a   on   with   the

Mom is on the raft.

Mom sits on a soft rag.

Dad is on the raft.

Dad sits on a soft mat.

Mom sits with Dad on the raft.

Lesson Sheet 20 (page 1)

h

g h o r s t

a f h m g o

hats	hot	frog	fog	hid	hot	gas	grass	get
(4)	(3)	(4)	(3)	(3)	(3)	(3)	(4)	(3)

Tim	trim
(3)	(4)

d o h g r s

t m h i r g

soft   hid

fog   frog

hot   hogs

mast   hat

from   with   was

the

Dot is a frog.

Dot sits in the fog.

Dot got a hat.

Tim the dog sat on Dot's hat.

Tim hid from Dot in the fog.

Lesson Sheet 21 (page 1)

h o r g h a F

i o s t f s d

Tim's	raft	digs	ham	got	hat	grass	get	frog
(4)	(4)	(4)	(3)	(3)	(3)	(4)	(3)	(4)

h g h o s h d

a f h m d i a

had   fog

frog   mat

mast   digs

raft   dogs

is   from   was

the

Tom the dog sat on soft rags.

Tom had a ham with him on the soft rags.

Tom got fat from the ham.

Lesson Sheet 22 (page 1)

| c |

h   c   g   o   c   r

d   h   c   f   a   t   c

Scott (4)	trim (4)	Mac (3)	cots (4)	cost (4)	last (4)	ill (2)	dress (4)	still (4)

h   o   r   c   g   h   i

c   a   h   c   a   i   o

Dot tag

Mac cats

sac cots

last grass

has   is   was

the   A   from

Mac is a cat.

Mac has a hat with dots.

The rim on Mac's hat sags.

A rat sits in Mac's hat.

Lesson Sheet 23 (page 1)

c h o g a D m

i f r a T c s

soft	trim	Scott	grass	trot	mill	dress	red	glad
(4)	(4)	(4)	(4)	(4)	(3)	(4)	(3)	(4)

h c g o a c r

s h a f c t o

ham   rot

trim   grass

him   had

cot   cost

is   was   has   a

with   the   from

Mac the cat sits on the cot.

Mac is Scott's cat.

Scott sits on the cot with Mac.

"Scat, cat!"

Mac trots off.

Lesson Sheet 24 (page 1)

l

c l h m l t G

i l o d f l a

grill	cost	hams	hill	lot	doll	last	cast	dog
(4)	(4)	(4)	(3)	(3)	(3)	(4)	(4)	(3)

fill	fell
(3)	(3)

c h o g a D m

i f r a T c s

Activity 4

mill   sand

lit   doll

hill   ran

last   still

Activity 5

is   was   has   a

with   the   from

The mill was on the hill.

Gill ran the mill.

The mill was a doll mill.

Gill's last doll was ill.

The mill was still.

Is the doll still ill?

Lesson Sheet 25 (page 1)

e

l e m t e s o

n r f e g l h

get	fit	hit	hats	dress	egg	less	Meg	red
(3)	(3)	(3)	(4)	(4)	(2)	(3)	(3)	(3)

e c l o a s t

r i f g h l e

red · · ·   ram · · ·

lots · · · ·   dress · · · · ·

him · · ·   stand · · · · ·

doll · · ·   get · · ·

because   is   was

a   the   with   has

Meg has a red dress. The dress has lots of dots.

Meg got the dress because it cost less.

Mom hems the dress because it sags. "Stand still, Meg!"

Lesson Sheet 26 (page 1)

e l m f e s i

l r a c r e d

bell	fib	crept	clot	bed	nest	plop	rob	rib
(3)	(3)	(5)	(4)	(3)	(4)	(4)	(3)	(3)

e l g m t s T

r f l c e a o

red	rat
rim	fit
leg	glad
dress	got

because   is   was

with   has   a

Meg has a doll with a red dress.

The doll has a red dress because Meg has a red dress.

Meg got the doll at Gill's mill.

Meg is with Gill at the doll mill.

Gill is glad because Meg got the doll.

Lesson Sheet 27 (page 1)

n

n d e s n o l i

c n d m f r n i

tin	ribs	best	sand	class	run	ran	Fred	Fran
(3)	(4)	(4)	(4)	(4)	(3)	(3)	(4)	(4)

beg	trim
(3)	(4)

n l f m g t

c d n e l a n

let   lot

lost   dress

red   rid

get   left

he   from   is

was   because

Ted lost Mom's red hat.

He set it on the raft.

Did Fred get it?

Did Meg get it?

Did Sam get it?

Ted is sad and Mom is red hot!

Lesson Sheet 28 (page 1)

b

e b n c a b n

o b n f m t b

bell	dog	bats	drift	craft	sells	sob	Fred	did
(3)	(3)	(4)	(5)	(5)	(4)	(3)	(4)	(3)

b c n e s b o

c b s d m f r

Activity 4

lost   red

bell   left

trim   bent

get   bat

Activity 5

because   is   was

has   from   with   he

Dan is a man with a big hat.

Fran is a trim cat.

Dot is a big rat.

Fran and Dot sat on a rag on the hot, hot, sand with Dan.

He got a tan.

Fran and Dot got red, not tan.

Dot and Fran left Dan on the hot, hot sand.

Lesson Sheet 29 (page 1)

n b e T a o n G

D t s b e a t T

slob	raft	glad	class	big	bog	dog	and	went
(4)	(4)	(4)	(4)	(3)	(3)	(3)	(3)	(4)

m n h l g n r

i o a e b t

big   frog

raft   hits

glad   bog

drifts   log

he   is   was   a

with   because   has

Ned is a big, fat frog.

He is with the class on a raft in a bog.

The raft drifts on and on.

The raft hits a log.

The frog hits the bog.

Ned is glad.

The class is sad.

Lesson Sheet 30 (page 1)

W

n w b e w l t

a w s D i n e

wet	swam	swim	slob	brim	tent	craft	fell	grand
(3)	(4)	(4)	(4)	(3)	(3)	(5)	(3)	(5)

n w e T a w o

G D t w b a

Lesson Sheet 30 (page 2)

Activity 4

went   raft

craft   band

swim   grin

frills   off

Activity 5

to   he   was   is

from   because

Dad ran in a crafts tent to get Mom a gift. He got Mom a grand hat with frills.

It had a big brim and a red band. Mom sat on a raft with the grand hat on. Mom got the hat wet because it fell off the raft.

Lesson Sheet 31 (page 1)

p

w p n f p l e

h p i b m t g c

nest	strap	plop	swift	pill	pull	drill	grand	grin
(4)	(5)	(4)	(5)	(3)	(3)	(4)	(5)	(4)

wet	wept
(3)	(4)

w n p w b e w l

a w s p D i m n

tin   twin

top   flips

wet   west

stop   flop

are   from   with

is   was   because   a

Peg and Greg are twin tots. Peg and Greg hop on top of cots.

Mom and Pop are hot because the twins are to nap, not hop. The twins' hops stop.

Lesson Sheet 32 (page 1)

p w n f p l e h

w i d b e m w t

drip	doll	band	step	bags	west	plan	cops	swift
(4)	(3)	(4)	(4)	(4)	(4)	(4)	(4)	(5)

stop	wept	spill
(4)	(4)	(4)

p w p n f l e h

p i b m t c o i

Peg   sled

helps   twig

blast   step

plop   flop

web   lands

from   is   was   are

with   a   because

Peg has a red sled. Will helps Peg drag the sled to the hill top. Peg and Will blast off.

Peg and Will hit a log and flip off the sled. Plop! Peg lands in a web and Will lands on a twig.

Lesson Sheet 33 (page 1)

---

ing

p e r ing b a e

ing n m h g ing d r

---

nap	napping	hop	hopping	plan	planning	grabs	dripping	swing
(3)	(4)	(3)	(4)	(4)	(5)	(5)	(5)	(3)

left	land	pond
(4)	(4)	(4)

---

ing w n ing p e h

d b ing m t g o

Lesson Sheet 33 (page 2)

Activity 4

hop   hopping

nap   napping

plop   drip

dripping   grabs

slips   rots

Activity 5

she   the   is   was

with   are   she   he

© 2001 by Sopris West. All rights reserved. This page may not be reproduced or reprinted without the express written permission of the publisher. Product code 142TDP.

The frog is napping on a log in the pond. Pam is planning to nab the frog. She grabs a net and slips to the log. She swings the net. Bam!

The frog plops into the pond and swims to land. Pam is left in the pond, dripping wet.

Lesson Sheet 34 (page 1)

ch

ing   p   i   ch   w   T   g

e   ch   G   e   i   r   ch   r

ranch	west	string	lost	hopping	hop	ants	chomp	ranch
(4)	(4)	(4)	(4)	(4)	(3)	(4)	(4)	(4)

chess	twig	went
(3)	(4)	(4)

ing   ch   p   ing   f   a   e

ing   n   m   g   ing   ch   o

Activity 4

west   cab

Chad   helps

went   trip

con   smell

Activity 5

They   he   is   was

because   to   they

Chad the cat went on a trip to the west with Ann.

They got to San Fran and got lost.

They got in a cab with a con man.

Chad smells a rat!

ch ing sh i p r o

ch d c t w m ing

hands	up	bump	bug	bag	big	beg	drag	bring
(5)	(2)	(4)	(3)	(3)	(3)	(3)	(4)	(3)

run	running
(3)	(4)

ch ing ch p i ch w

g ch G e i r ch

Lesson Sheet 35 (page 2)

hiss hands

drops clap

glad stops

limps chomp

They he is are

with because has

The con man stops the cab and robs Ann! He rips the bags in Ann's hands. Chad is mad. Hiss! Spit!

Chad chomps the con man's legs. The con man drops Ann's bags and limps off. Chad and Ann clap because they are glad.

Lesson Sheet 36 (page 1)

u

ch   u   ing   w   u

b   d   n   u   g   h   i

bigger	get	getting	under	glub	Chip	tub	swims	run
(4)	(3)	(4)	(4)	(4)	(3)	(3)	(5)	(3)

running	runner	runs
(4)	(4)	(4)

ch ing sh   p   r   o   ch

d   c   t   w   m   ing   o

chip   fell

flips   glub

hops   hopping

slug   lunch

| have | from | They |

he   have   a   is

Chip the bug fell in the tub. Plop! Rub a dub dub. Chip swims and bobs. He dips and flips.

Pug the slug hops into the tub with Chip. They have fun in the tub. Glub, glub, glub.

er

ch   er   ing   w   er

o   f   er   b   g

p   F   n   er   w

u   er   ch   ing   er

b   d   n   u   er   h

<u>her</u>   <u>bet</u>

<u>bett er</u>   <u>slim</u>

<u>swimm er</u>   <u>swimm ing</u>

<u>run</u>   <u>runn ing</u>

<u>runn er</u>   <u>helps</u>

| than | are | from | was |

because   they   is

Chet is a runner and Nell is a swimmer. Chet is a better runner than Nell, but she is a better swimmer than Chet.

Chet helps Nell run. Nell helps Chet swim. They are pals.

er u ch e ing

p d b i R l

r ch o e b p

er ch er ing w er

o f er b g n

best   stop

rich   bett er

big   bigg er

swim   hicc up

swimm ing   hicc upp ing

have   they   a   than   she

from   is   was   the

Chip and Pug are pals. They have fun in the tub because they are bugs.

They swim in the tub, but Chip is the better swimmer. Pug cannot swim well because he has hiccups.

Chip helps Pug to stop hiccupping. Can Pug swim well?

j

ing ch e u j p

j ch c n m er

er j u ch e ing

a w p d i R

er r j o i b

<u>j</u><u>og</u>   <u>j</u><u>ogg</u> <u>er</u>

<u>s</u><u>um</u>   <u>s</u><u>umm</u> <u>er</u>

<u>dump</u>   <u>bump</u>

<u>fast</u>   <u>fill</u>

<u>spill</u>   <u>stump</u>

| his | because | they |

she   was   with   has

have   are   from

Jill is a jogger. Jill runs faster than Bill. Jeff runs just as fast as Jill.

Jeff, Jill, and Bill are jogging in the hot summer sun. Jeff bumps his leg on a stump and has a spill.

Jill and Bill stop jogging and help Jeff get up. Jeff sits on a log and rests his leg.

Lesson Sheet 40 (page 1)

k

ing	k	p	l	e	w
n	er	r	g	k	o
k	j	er	j	u	ch
j	er	ing	ch	e	u
ch	c	n	m	er	r

<u>top</u>   <u>topp</u> <u>er</u>

<u>spill</u>   <u>milk</u>

<u>jump</u>   <u>jump</u> <u>ing</u>

<u>tilts</u>   <u>string</u>

<u>snags</u>   <u>sulk</u>

<u>swing</u>   <u>batt</u> <u>ing</u>

of   she   to   are   have   he

she   is   than   they   of

Topper the cat is batting at a string. He tilts a cup of milk and it spills on Kim's silk dress. Kim's dress is wet.

Topper snags the dress as he laps up the milk. Kim is mad because she is wet. She grabs him and plops him on the rug.

Topper sulks until he spots a jumping bug. He blasts off of the rug and steps on the bug.

ck

u	w	ck	r	er	g
l	k	ck	G	K	er
k	ck	j	k	er	u
ch	p	ing	e	w	k
g	k	ck	o	c	h

<u>Jack</u>   <u>pond</u>

<u>lunch</u>   <u>crunch</u>

<u>crack</u>   <u>crack</u> <u>ers</u>

<u>sack</u>   <u>snack</u>

<u>grabs</u>   <u>un</u> <u>pack</u>

of   his   he   she

are   to   because

Ken and Jack pack a lunch in a sack. They get to a big rock and unpack the sack. They munch on crackers and crunch on chips.

A bunch of ants are under the rock. They smell a snack and run to the top of the rock. Ken grabs his crackers; Jack grabs his chips. They run to the duck pond to have lunch.

Lesson Sheet 42 (page 1)

ck   ing   ch   c   b   j

o   er   w   b   e   ck

s   w   m   ch   ck   k

ck   c   ck   er   ing   k

u   w   ck   r   er   F

Jack   sick

job   back

grass   glad

crab   slip

frog   black

look   his   she   A

have   are   they   with

he   was

Jack digs in the sand under the hot sun. He digs and he digs and he digs. Bam! Pinch!

He is bit on the hand. He looks in the sand. AAAH! It's a big, red crab. The crab looks at Jack and grins — pinch, pinch.

Jack nabs the crab and puts it in a crab trap. The crab is mad, mad, mad. Pinch, pinch. The crab hits the trap with his fists, but he is stuck. That is much better for Jack.

ee

ck   ee   j   k   ee   ck

u   p   ee   ch   k   er

ee   c   j   p   r   b   o

ee   ck   ch   s   c   e

w   ee   k   er   c   u

t<u>ent</u>   <u>af</u><u>ter</u>

<u>meet</u>   <u>sleep</u>

<u>sleep</u><u>ing</u>   <u>duck</u>

<u>grass</u>   <u>green</u>

<u>pack</u>   <u>un</u><u>pack</u>

<u>set</u>   <u>sett</u><u>ing</u>

their   of   his   to   than

are   look   is   has

Ken and Jack meet on the green, green grass at the duck pond to munch their lunch.

After lunch, they need a nap. They set up their big green tent. They creep into the tent and unpack their sleeping bags. Ken and Jack slip into their sleeping bags. They sleep and sleep and sleep.

They slept well.

ea

ing	w	ee	h	ch	ing
o	ee	ea	ck	er	u	i
ea	ee	ck	u	p	ch
er	ea	m	ee	ea	o
ee	ck	ch	c	ea	ee

lots

tent

eat

eats

eat ing

drip

dripp ing

gut

get

feel

dream

peach

their   from   a   of

have   she   to

Ken and Jack are still sleeping in their big green tent. Ken has a dream. In his dream, he and Jack are eating lots and lots.

They have beans dripping with butter, peaches with cream, and lean ham. After eating the grand meal, Ken and Jack feel plump.

Ken gets up because his gut went "grrr." "It was just a dream!" he screams.

ea	ee	k	ck	n	ch
e	l	ing	ee	ch	h
w	er	m	e	i	ea	r
ea	ck	j	ee	k	ing
c	w	ea	ee	d	h	ch

<u>Ken</u>   <u>still</u>

<u>dream</u>   <u>grab</u>

<u>feels</u>   <u>reels</u>

<u>tell</u>   <u>just</u>

<u>scream</u>   <u>scream</u> <u>ing</u>

| I | is | are | their |

to   he   his   they

Ken and Jack are still in the tent. Ken is screaming, "It was just a dream!" Jack is mad. He tells Ken, "Stop screaming! I was sleeping!"

Ken tells Jack, "I feel weak. I need to eat." Ken leaps up. "Grab the rods and reels. Let's get dinner."

After dinner, Ken feels better, but Jack feels plump.

sh

sh	u	er	sh	c	ch
u	j	o	ch	i	ea
sh	ea	ee	b	p	ch
e	w	er	sh	i	e
ch	ea	d	sh	er	r

<u>fish</u>   <u>fish</u> <u>ing</u>

<u>swish</u>   <u>splish</u>

<u>splash</u>   <u>dock</u>

<u>bass</u>   <u>wish</u>

<u>chest</u>   <u>Chest</u> <u>er</u>

| for | his | to |

from   have   I

Chester the cat went fishing for lunch. He ran to the pond with his rod and reel. He sat on the dock and fished. He wished for a big bass.

Splash! He spotted a fin. Swish, splish, splash! "It's a bass! It's a bass!" Chester screamed.

Chester felt a tug on his rod. Chester tugged back and the bass landed on the dock. "Fish for lunch!"

aw

k	ea	ch	n	h
ee	j	ea	e	aw	ch
sh	ea	ck	ee	u
ing	u	o	n	b	w
u	j	aw	ch	ea	sh

<u>Chest</u>er   <u>weeds</u>

<u>trot</u>   <u>trott</u><u>ing</u>

<u>aw</u>ful   <u>paw</u>

<u>claw</u>   <u>crawl</u>

<u>sped</u>   <u>spill</u>

| over | she | his | A |

for   with   I   look

After lunch was over, Chester the cat sat in a seat on his lawn. He sat with a big glass of tea in his paw.

He sipped his tea with a straw. "Aw! It can't get better than this!" He looked at the fish swimming in the pond. He looked at a bug crawling over a tree.

He spotted Chet the awful dog running over to him. "Hiss!" Chester screamed. He jumped up, spilling his tea. He lept up and sped off.

Lesson Sheet 48 (page 1)

aw sh j er ck er

ing u ch k sh

ea b sh n er l

sh aw er ing aw

ea c aw ee ea e

d aw ch k c sh

kit   kitten

lap   lapped

lick   licking

munch   munched

lawn   clean

finish   crawl

I   his   was   are

because   for   over

Chester the cat and Josh the kitten got up at ten. For brunch, Chester munched on raw eggs and fish, and Josh lapped milk in a dish.

After they finished eating, Chester cleaned his paws and Josh licked his claws. After cleaning paws and licking claws, Chester and Josh romped on the lawn.

They leaped over logs, crawled under bushes, and hopped on a seesaw. Chester and Josh had fun on the lawn.

ur

j	ur	i	u	ch	ea
k	p	C	d	sh	ch
aw	sh	j	er	ck
ing	u	ch	k	sh
w	ea	b	sh	ir

surf   swam

beach   burn

skin   sand

dawn   jogged

curl   curled

as   when

are   from   she

Nan and Kim went to the beach at dawn. They jogged on the beach and hunted for shells in the sand.

After hunting for shells, jogging, and surfing, Nan and Kim curled up on the sand to rest. They fell asleep in the sun.

Nan and Kim's skin turned red as they slept. When they got up, they had bad burns.

ir

ing	ir	er	aw	ir
ir	aw	ur	u	sh
ch	sh	ur	ck	ing
j	ir	i	u	ch	ea	ur
k	p	C	d	sh	ch

bird   burn

went   sir

keep   keep er

beach   cream

shirt   skirt

| said | I | is | for | when |

as   said   over   their

Nan and Kim's skin hurt because they had bad sunburns. They put on their shirts and skirts. They left the beach.

They went shopping for skin cream. They went into a shop and met Chuck the shopkeeper.

Nan said to Chuck, "Sir, I have a bad sunburn. I need the best skin cream in the shop."

ir   sh   aw   ur   u

er   ing   u   ir   w

l   e   er   r   h   sh

ing   ir   er   aw   ir

ir   aw   ur   u   sh   ch

<u>raw</u>   <u>rub</u>

<u>rubbed</u>   <u>rubb</u> ing

<u>shirt</u>   <u>skirt</u>

<u>beach</u>   <u>burn</u>

<u>burned</u>   <u>bawled</u>

next   over   for   I

of   said   when   from

Kim and Nan had bad sunburns. When they left the beach, their legs, hands, and backs felt hot and looked red. It hurt just having on their shirts and skirts.

When they got to Chuck's shop, they bawled, "It hurts! It hurts! Sob! Sob! Sob!"

Chuck handed Nan the best cream for bad sunburns. The girls rubbed the cream on their red, red burned skin. It felt raw.

"This cream helps my skin not feel hot," said Kim. Nan just said, "Aw, much better!"

th

ir	th	ur	ck
er	th	ing	ch	k
er	b	l	d	j	th
ch	sh	aw	ur	th
er	ing	u	th	w	p

<u>teeth</u>   <u>rott</u><u>ing</u>

<u>spots</u>   <u>dent</u><u>ist</u>

<u>hab</u><u>it</u>   <u>black</u>

<u>mom</u>   <u>feel</u><u>ing</u>

<u>thick</u>   <u>sweets</u>

your   from   their

when   I   look   than

Trent eats lots of sweets. This bad habit rots his teeth. Trent's teeth have black spots on them.

His mom tells him, "Your teeth are rotting!" She sends him to the dentist.

The dentist drills the rotting spots, then fills them in. Next, the dentist tells Trent, "Brush your teeth after each meal and eat less sweets!"

ou

| th | ou | ir | sh | ou |

| aw | ch | p | th | ou | er |

| ir | th | ur | ou | ck |

| er | ou | ing | ch | k |

| ou | b | l | d | j | ou |

<u>shout</u>   <u>shout</u> <u>ed</u>

<u>eat</u> <u>ing</u>   <u>ad</u> <u>mit</u>

<u>proud</u>   <u>pout</u>

<u>sweet</u>   <u>Trent</u>

<u>drill</u>   <u>drilled</u>

| my | too | for | have |

when   said   from

Trent shouted, "Ouch!" when the dentist drilled his teeth. "That hurts my mouth," he said.

He pouted when the dentist said, "Brush your teeth after each meal and eat less sweets!"

But Trent was too proud to admit, "My teeth feel clean. I will stop eating sweets."

Trent went to his mom and said, "I found out that I need to brush my teeth after each meal. My habit of eating sweets must stop, too."

"I am proud," said Trent's mom.

ou	th	ir	aw	ur
th	ing	ck	ea	j
th	ou	ir	sh	ou
aw	ch	p	th	ou
h	ch	o	e	ing	ou

<u>kick</u> <u>ing</u>   <u>eat</u> <u>ing</u>

<u>a</u> <u>dopt</u>   <u>a</u> <u>dopt</u> <u>ed</u>

<u>spott</u> <u>ed</u>   <u>bath</u> <u>tub</u>

<u>black</u>   <u>pound</u>

<u>couch</u>   <u>a</u> <u>sleep</u>

house   your   from

to   over   for   I   of

For kicking his habit of eating sweets, Trent's mom let him get a hound at the pound. Trent adopted Mack the tan and black spotted hound.

They went to Trent's house. "This is my house and it is your house too," said Trent to Mack.

Trent said, "Mack, your fur smells. Hop in the bathtub and I'll clean you."

After Mack had his bath, he felt glad. He jumped on the couch and fell asleep. Trent felt glad, too.

ow

th   ir   sh   D   j

n   ow   ou   ea   p

ou   ow   I   w   u

ee   ow   ch   aw

er   ur   ow   ing   g

dapp<u>er</u>   ent<u>er</u>

<u>en</u> <u>tered</u>   frown

gown   dressed

<u>can</u> <u>not</u>   <u>wedd</u> <u>ing</u>

<u>down</u> <u>town</u>   <u>flow</u> <u>er</u>

shimm<u>er</u>   shimm<u>er</u> <u>ing</u>

| were |

my   to

your   I

Dapper Dan picked flowers for his best girl Jan. Dan and Jan were to wed in the big church downtown.

Dan dashed to Jan's house to hand her the flowers. Jan was getting dressed in her shimmering wedding gown.

Jan's mom stopped Dan as he entered the house. She frowned and said, "You cannot see Jan now. She is getting dressed in her wedding gown."

ar

ow	ar	ou	sh	g
ar	th	ir	ck	ar
k	er	aw	ing	o
ch	c	o	p	ck	ea
j	ar	I	G	er

flow<u>ers</u>   <u>stand</u>

<u>stand</u><u>ing</u>   <u>wed</u>

<u>wedd</u><u>ing</u>   <u>church</u>

<u>gar</u><u>den</u>   <u>pick</u><u>et</u>

<u>a</u><u>bout</u>   <u>darn</u>

from   were   is

said   too   was   your

"Darn," said Dan when Jan's mom stopped him from seeing Jan.

He handed the flowers to Jan's mom, hopped in the car, and sped to the church. Dan's best man, Bart, was standing in the church's garden. Bart had the wedding ring in his pocket.

Bart said to Dan, "Park your car and get in the church. The wedding is about to start."

ow	ir	ou	er	ck
D	sh	aw	th	ee	i
ar	ow	ar	ou	sh
ch	c	ur	p	ow
k	er	aw	ing	ar

<u>down</u> <u>town</u>   <u>gather</u>

<u>ga</u> <u>thered</u>   <u>with</u> <u>out</u>

<u>wedd</u> <u>ing</u>   <u>block</u>

<u>blocked</u>   <u>asked</u>

<u>round</u>   <u>a</u> <u>round</u>

| you | as | from | of |

for   to   their

Lesson Sheet 57 (page 3)

Activity 4

A crowd gathered at the downtown church for Dan and Jan's wedding. Cars were parked up and down the street.

"Jan is not at the church!" shouted Bart. "How can the wedding start without Jan?"

The parked cars were blocking the street and Jan's car was stuck far from the church. "You and I will have to get out of the car and run to the church," said Jan's mom.

They darted around the parked cars and got to the church just as the Wedding March started.

SOPRIS
WEST

Together We Can!
ClassWide Peer Tutoring to Improve Basic Academic Skills

Charles Greenwood, Ph.D.; Joseph Delquadri, Ph.D.; and Judith Carta, Ph.D.
Grades 1–8

Drill and memorization become a fun part of the school day, off-task behavior is reduced, and practice time increases when you implement this research-based, peer-tutoring program in your classroom. ClassWide Peer Tutoring groups individual class members into tutor-tutee pairs who work together on two competing teams. Tutees earn points for their team by responding to the tasks presented by their tutors; tutors earn points from the teacher, depending on their correct implementation of the tutoring role. The result is significant academic gain—even among students at risk for academic failure—in any content area that involves memorization and drill. This resource comes with easy-to-follow directions, reproducible masters, and four 20" x 30" dry-erase charts (Team/Partners, Test Scores, and two Team Points Charts). Minimal time requirements, frequent testing, immediate error correction, and easy implementation make this a winning resource. (G95SET)

Read Well

Fully Decodable Text With Rich Literature

Marilyn Sprick, M.S.; Lisa Howard, B.A.; and Ann Fidanque, M.A.
Grades 1 and Remedial 2–3
(K with age-appropriate modifications)

Build the essential foundation in reading and comprehension proficiency for your high-, average-, and low-performing beginning readers. *Read Well* is a field-tested reading program that combines research-based skills instruction with a strong literature foundation. Appropriate for both natural readers and students who need systematic instruction, *Read Well* allows you to:

- Deliver comprehensive reading instruction easily
- Improve reading comprehension
- Increase student's reading independence
- Make teaching more fun!

Read Well enables first grade and remedial second and third grade students to master phonemic awareness skills, sound-symbol recognition, blending, rhyming patterns, multisyllabic words, and fluency in passage reading. *Read Well* provides:

- Fully decodable student text
- Rich thematic content (e.g., frog facts, metamorphosis, flight)
- A variety of genres (e.g., poetry, nonfiction)
- Mastery-based assessment
- Integrated writing exercises (written retells and reports)

Each unit includes six stories, with odd-numbered stories in the unique "duet" format and even-numbered stories in the "solo" format. All 38 units feature suggested literature to be read aloud, daily decoding lessons, and narrative expository passage reading. *Read Well* meets the needs of schools in search of an affordable and effective bridge to literature-based programs.

All materials that require student writing are available in plain or slanted text.

- Plain Text Sample: The quick brown fox jumps over the lazy dog.
- Slanted Text Sample: *The quick brown fox jumps over the lazy dog.*

(G93INST-P, Plain Text Version)
(G93INST-S, Slanted Text Version)